BRASSY BIT *of* AGING CRUMPET

ALSO BY MARY WALSH

Crying for the Moon

BRASSY
BIT
of
AGING
CRUMPET

Mary Walsh

Brassy Bit of Aging Crumpet
Copyright © 2026 by Mary Walsh.
All rights reserved.

Published by Harper Avenue, an imprint of HarperCollins Publishers Ltd

FIRST EDITION

Some names and identifying characteristics have been changed.

No part of this book may be used or reproduced in any manner whatsoever without written permission.

Without limiting the exclusive rights of any author, contributor or the publisher of this publication, any unauthorized use of this publication to train generative artificial intelligence (AI) technologies is expressly prohibited. HarperCollins also exercise their rights under Article 4(3) of the Digital Single Market Directive 2019/790 and expressly reserve this publication from the text and data mining exception.

"September 1, 1939," copyright 1940 and © renewed 1968 by W. H. Auden; from *Collected Poems* by W. H. Auden, edited by Edward Mendelson. Used by permission of Random House, an imprint and division of Penguin Random House LLC. All rights reserved.

HarperCollins books may be purchased for educational, business, or sales promotional use through our Special Markets Department.

HarperCollins Publishers Ltd
Bay Adelaide Centre, East Tower
22 Adelaide Street West, 41st Floor
Toronto, Ontario, Canada
M5H 4E3

www.harpercollins.ca

HarperCollins Publishers
Macken House, 39/40 Mayor Street Upper
Dublin 1, D01 C9W8, Ireland
www.harpercollins.com

Library and Archives Canada Cataloguing in Publication

Title: Brassy bit of aging crumpet / Mary Walsh.
Names: Walsh, Mary, 1952- author
Identifiers: Canadiana (print) 20250330539 | Canadiana (ebook) 20250330571 | ISBN 9781443471978 (hardcover) | ISBN 9781443471985 (EPUB)
Subjects: LCSH: Walsh, Mary, 1952- | LCSH: Television actors and actresses—Canada—Biography. | LCSH: Recovering alcoholics—Canada—Biography. | LCSH: Newfoundland and Labrador—Biography. | CSH: Women authors, Canadian (English)—21st century—Biography. | CSH: Authors, Canadian (English)—21st century—Biography. | LCGFT: Autobiographies.
Classification: LCC PN2308.W35 A3 2026 | DDC 791.4502/8092—dc23

Printed and bound in the United States of America

26 27 28 29 30 LBC 5 4 3 2 1

*For my husband Don Nichol and my son Jesse Cox,
with love and gratitude.*

*Faces along the bar
cling to their average day.
The lights must never go out
the music must always play [. . .]
lest we should see where we are,
lost in a haunted wood,
children afraid of the night
who have never been happy or good.*

—W. H. AUDEN

Contents

Preface xi

THE LITTLE GIRL WHO GREW UP
    NEXT DOOR TO HER FAMILY 1

MOM 25

CARTER'S HILL 43

COME HOME YEAR 49

MAKIN' TIME WITH THE YANKS 77

WRITE WHAT YOU KNOW 95

CODCO 105

NEWFOUNDLAND 131

CANADA 141

22 MINUTES 149

TAKING HOSTAGES 169

UNTITLED 185

CHANGE 199

BRASSY BIT OF AGING CRUMPET 207

Acknowledgements 217

Preface

WHEN I SET OUT TO WRITE THESE ESSAYS, THE EDITOR at HarperCollins suggested that they might look and read a little like Nora Ephron's collection *I Feel Bad About My Neck*. I love Nora Ephron. In the early 1970s, I remember reading her pieces in *Esquire* magazine and, along with Joan Didion, she became one of my major literary heroines. So I thought, "Great." And I went out and bought and reread *I Feel Bad About My Neck*, and to this day it's still a great book of essays—so blithe and so breezy, and yet able to say so much with such a light touch. My heart sank. I thought, "I can't do this. My life is so different than this. I am neither blithe nor breezy, nor bouncy at all. I'm more like a loud thud."

Nora Ephron talks about parenting and about how when kids leave for college you should change their rooms into dens right away, for fears they'd be tempted to move back in. My own struggles with parenting have felt way heftier, weightier, way more unmanageable than redecorating their bedrooms. And I thought that I would never be able to be light about all the sadness and heartbreak and failure I feel around so many parts of my life. I thought there were way too many hard words starting with "A"—abuse, abandonment, alcoholism—littering my life for me to ever try to write a series of bright and breezy pieces about it.

Yet, as I sat down to write the first essay, I read this quote from G. K. Chesterton: "Angels can fly because they take themselves so lightly." And I had a kind of epiphanic moment then, almost a spiritual awakening, and I thought, "Why not?" Why not try to approach things with a lighter heart and a lighter hand? That quote seemed like a clear message to me. So that's it then, I thought, for the rest of this book I was going to lighten up and calm the fuck down. Because yes, I was abandoned, and yes, I went through most of the abuses, including alcohol and drugs, and I could list them all for you, but to what end? I'm not going to do it, because these days I feel like I'm finally beginning to rise up off my self-pity pot, but fair warning, I probably still have the print of that pity pot on my arse.

Why do people write memoirs? Or even essays that are memoir-ish? I'm struggling, because if we are honest, or at least if I am honest, my life is just chock-a-block full of the most humiliating and embarrassing situations, and failures. Triumphs, too, of course. But sadly, the triumphs often led to smug grandiosity. Oh, if I only had the courage to share the vast acreage of my feelings, all the way from my deepest shame to the heights of self-satisfied big-shot-ism. They say the unexamined life is not worth living, but hey, is the examined one any more worthwhile? If I just look at the things that happened outside of myself, it's not that difficult to tell the story, but when I'm forced to look into the muck and the misery of my own heart and soul, I rebel, I don't want to go there. I just don't want to talk about it. How small I've been sometimes, how petty and mean-minded, and envious, and covetous, and greedy. Has anyone else trod this particularly mortifying path through their life? Perhaps everyone suffers from these ailments of the heart. But they don't always cop to it, do they?

Trying to write an honest and straightforward take on my life has also put me in the humbling position of realizing what an ingrate I've been, how many people have helped me, have carried me, have taken care of me, how much I have to be grateful for, and how little time I have spent practicing that gratitude. Mostly I've mimped and moaned about what I don't have, about how nobody loves me, about how abandoned I've been, and yet, when I think of all the care people have afforded me, all the love, all the time and energy, the light comes on, the sun comes up, the world becomes a place full of a thousand tendernesses, and I am so grateful for the life I've been granted to live, for everything—for the failures, for the triumphs, for the blessings and the troubles, for all of it.

BRASSY BIT of AGING CRUMPET

The Little Girl Who Grew Up Next Door to Her Family

ONCE UPON A TIME THERE WAS A LITTLE GIRL WHO grew up next door to her family. This little girl was raised by her two maiden aunts and an invalid uncle on 9 Carter's Hill. Let's call that the "lace curtain" Irish section of the house. Her parents and her seven brothers and sisters—Kevin, Michael, Madonna, Laura, Carol, Frank, and Greg—all lived at 7 Carter's Hill. We will call that the "shanty" Irish section. Now, number seven and number nine were actually just one large house, one large house divided, each with its own entrance. The mom and the dad and the seven brothers and sisters all lived in the basement and on part of the first floor, and the little girl and her aunt Mae, her aunt Phine, and her uncle Jack lived on the in-all-ways more lofty second and third floor of the house.

The little girl had been banished from her real home when she was just eight months old.* She had gotten pneumonia and spent some weeks in the hospital, but when she came home, her parents determined their house was too cold and damp.** So they sent her upstairs to 9 Carter's Hill, where it was warmer and drier. She was only supposed to stay there until she was fully recovered, yet for reasons the little girl never understood—and always felt heartbroken about (and spent a small fortune on hard liquor and Class-A drugs to forget)—they never came to get her back.***

Of course, that little girl is me, but I never wanted to acknowledge that sad story as my story. I never wanted to be that Little Girl. I wanted to be a much better little girl—a little girl who no one would ever abandon. As long as I can remember, I disassociated myself from that poor little abandoned girl. I was still trapped though in a lifetime of feeling sad about her. It was a very odd way to grow up, living so close to your entire family but also completely separate from them. It left me feeling confused and confounded and never believing that I belonged anywhere.

Downstairs in Mom and Dad's place, there were drinkers, fornicators, and fighters; yellers, screechers, and furniture breakers.

---

* I know I promised to lighten the f up, but then I wrote this and I kind of had to get it off my chest. Now I know some people have much better childhoods than mine, and a whole lot of people have way worse ones (including my siblings) but this is me, as far as I can understand it anyway.

** They say that lung trouble is related to loss and grief, but how in the name of God could I be grief stricken when I was only eight months old?

*** What, did they forget about me? I was just upstairs, for Christ's sake!

Mom's crowd was often from around the bay,* and they were big drinkers. Dad's crowd was up from the longshore,** and oddly enough they were big drinkers, too. Downstairs there were also adulterers, thieves, firebugs, police cars, Black Marias, fire trucks, china cabinets thrown down the stairs,*** teenage pregnancies (quite a few of them, actually), suicide attempts, and unexplained deaths. Christmas downstairs had a loud, nightmarish quality to it, and Easter pretty well went unnoticed.

Upstairs with Aunt Mae, Aunt Phine, and Uncle Jack, it was quiet, but an uneasy kind of quiet—the kind of quiet you feel sometimes when you look at a Christopher Pratt or Alex Colville painting. The kind of quiet that says that something awful is just about to happen. Looking back, it's obvious to me now that all of the grownups upstairs were probably suffering from some kind of depression. Aunt Mae (my dad's stepsister), the least depressed of all of them, had lost a leg when she was just four years old and always talked about how she was only half there. She was unmarried and deeply regretted that she had never had an opportunity to dance or skate. Uncle Jack (Aunt Mae's brother and Dad's stepbrother), also unmarried, had suffered a blood clot through the brain and nine strokes that paralyzed his right side, leaving him severely depressed. Aunt Phine (my father's real sister, Aunt Mae and Uncle Jack's stepsister) had married later in life. Her husband tragically died two months after the ceremony, and just one week after Aunt Phine

---

* Townies, as people from St. John's call themselves, believe that any place "outside the overpass" is around the bay, and all people who live there are automatically called baymen. When I was growing up, Townies were very contemptuous of baymen. That attitude, thank God, has radically changed.

** Longshore work refers to work along the shore or on the waterfront.

*** More on this later.

had finally finished the massive cleanup of his house (where he'd lived as a bachelor for thirty years). As an exhausted, sick-to-death-of-house-cleaning widow, she had to move back in with her stepbrother and stepsister to keep house and look after them, and eventually to care for me as well. All of these things made Aunt Phine, if not depressed, then certainly very angry.

Oh yes, and upstairs we got down on our knees and said the Rosary every night, and not just the five Sorrowful, Glorious, or Joyful mysteries of the Rosary either. After we got through all of those Hail-a Marys, Our Fathers, and Glory Bes, the crowd upstairs felt the need to add a whole bunch of extra prayers at the end of and on top of all those previous intersessions. I remember one interminable prayer wherein we pleaded for God to protect us from every disease known to humanity, many of which had never been seen on the island of Newfoundland. Oh, we prayed to ward off cholera, malaria, scabies, dengue fever, chaga disease, leprosy, typhoid fever, sickle cell anemia, spina bifida, stone man syndrome, muscular dystrophy, cystic fibrosis, and hemophilia, as well as, of course, the more familiar illnesses like tuberculosis, polio, pneumonia, and influenza—and that's only the half of them.

Oh God, I was so bored during that ceaseless Rosary. I thought my head was going to blow right off my shoulders. And every night before sleep, Aunt Phine would inevitably drench me with holy water to cleanse me of impure (read: sexual) thoughts. She would also recite this prayer to protect me from all other lurking evils:* "Please purify me Lord, banish all of the forces of evil from me: banish from me all spells, witchcraft,

---

* If not this exact prayer, then one just as terrifying.

black magic, curses, the evil eye, diabolic infestations, oppressions, possessions, all that is evil and sinful, and consign them into the everlasting hell where they will be crushed under the heel of the Immaculate Virgin Mary." It was a miracle that, as a child, I ever managed to strike a wink of sleep after the terrifying images that particular prayer put into my head.

And while we're on the subject of boring, upstairs we always had the same meals, over and over and over again. On Sunday, we ate roast, Monday leftovers, Tuesday stew, Wednesday fish, Thursday salt meat, Friday fish again, Saturday sausages, leading inevitably back to the Sunday roast and on and on and on and never changing. I know it's not right to complain; they were good meals, and nutritious, too, I guess (and meals that Aunt Phine never tired of reminding me I was lucky to have). But I wanted food for kids, fun food, like the kind they had on television. I always wanted what I thought all the other little girls were having. I wanted a tin of bright orange Chef Boyardee, straight from the can. I wanted SpaghettiOs, peanut butter and jam sandwiches, and what my two best friends next door, Boopy and Tishy, used to eat—slices of white bread, thick margarine, and a big heaping of white sugar on top. But I always had an orange, or something similarly healthful and boring.

God alone knows what Mom and them were eating downstairs. I knew it was unlikely they were on any kind of rigid meal schedule. Nothing was scheduled downstairs.

Upstairs, the menu also featured plenty of beef tea (similar to bone broth), brandy flips, eggs in a glass, custards, and Spanish creams. Bland, strengthening food for people with illnesses, because upstairs there was sickness: strokes, kidney stones, blood clots through the brain, arthritis, heart attacks, fits of depression, and various cancer scares. All of this was profoundly alarming to me, and what was even more terrifying was when the priest would come to give Uncle Jack Extreme Unction, or the Last Rites.

When I was little, every time I turned around there was a priest at our house, often arriving just before the ambulance. Usually it was handsome Father Conroy, who was a friend of the family.* Father Conroy was tall, thin, and bespectacled. I found him extremely attractive in his long black dress and the cute black hat with the pom-pom he always wore. He walked so quietly but with such urgency through our quiet, unrelievedly tense house. He said the Last Rites in a sonorous, powerful voice that I liked to think of as his priest voice: "Remember man that thou art dust and onto dust thou shalt return." I think Uncle Jack must have received the Last Rites at least twelve times, and each time I found it even more alarming than the one before. Afterward, Aunt Mae and Aunt Phine were sad and distant for days.

Christmas upstairs was quiet. Often Uncle Jack returned home for the holidays from the Waterford Hospital for Mental and Nervous Disorders, or "the Mental," as everyone called it, or in his last years, the nursing home. I was always warned that any loud noise could startle Uncle Jack into . . . well, what exactly, I never knew. And I was never brave enough to make enough noise to find out.

---

* Sometimes Father Conroy and his mother even came up to the country to visit us. Our shack was only nine miles from our place on Carter's Hill. As soon as school was over, Aunt Mae, Aunt Phine, Uncle Jack, and I would pile into Frank Dunn's taxicab. He drove for Radio Cabs, and he was our regular taximan and driver. Aunt Phine, Uncle Jack, and I would stay there all summer, but poor, brave, stalwart Aunt Mae would limp up the road each morning to catch a bus to her job at the Provincial Department of Public Works.

One Christmas when, for some reason, Uncle Jack was not allowed to come home (which was a bit of a relief to me, although I was riddled with guilt for feeling that relief), my two aunties, who were always particularly low-minded all through the twelve days of Christmas, were even more glum than usual. They went to see Uncle Jack at the Mental. Anyone under the age of twelve was strictly prohibited from visiting, so for the first year ever, I spent Christmas afternoon with my real family. I was happy not to go to the Mental, and to spend the afternoon with the crowd downstairs. That Christmas, Santa Claus brought me two baby dollies, and I was delighted. One was the baby dolly that all the girls in school wanted for Christmas; she actually wet herself.

That afternoon, I discovered that my two brothers, Frank and Greg, who were twelve and six, had gotten one pair of leather mitts from Santa Claus. One pair to share between them. They spent the afternoon pretending they were boxing gloves and using them to beat the shit out of each other. My little brother Greg explained to me why they had received so little from Santa. "Santy Claus never got a chance to leave that much because last night I was up late drinkin' with Dad—yeah, drinkin'—with Dad and Jack Costello. Santy Claus come down over dem stairs and I picked up a hockey puck and I said, 'Get da fuck up over dem stairs,' and I let 'er drift and I got him, too, right on the side of the head. He dropped these"—Greg pointed to the mitts—"and den he took off and he never come back either." At the time, I didn't really understand why that story made me feel so sad, and why a part of me wanted to give my brother one of my baby dollies. I didn't. I wanted them too much.

Now, usually when I tell the story I say that I gave my brother the baby doll that wet herself, and that he tore the head right off that dolly and threw it at me, and then, holding the doll's headless body aloft, said, "Hey missus, your baby just pissed itself, and now it's dead." To me, it was a better story, but that's not really what happened. Greg never tore the heads off any of my dolls, but it is true that my brothers got only one pair of mitts for Christmas, and Greg did tell me how he had driven Santa Claus away and that was why they got so little. As is always the case, when you grow up in the party house and there's excessive alcohol involved, Christmas turns out to be just another excuse for the grown-ups to drink even more.

Easter for me involved receiving a Terry's Chocolate Egg. It broke in two halves and contained real chocolates inside, all tastefully done up in a lavender tin, tied together with a mauve ribbon. It was the kind of chocolate egg I always imagined an old lady would love to get on Easter morning, and I knew even then I would be ungrateful and small if I weren't thrilled by it, but I wasn't. At Easter, I wanted what I imagined everybody else had. In my mind's eye, I saw all the other St. John's children having a high-spirited, laughter-filled Easter Egg hunt with their siblings and their young, vibrant, decidedly not depressed parents. The other problem I had with Easter was Holy Week, which consisted of endless churchgoing that was even more grim than usual. Everything in the church was wrapped up in black cloth: the statues, the altar, and even the monstrance. It was as if the physical church itself was deep in mourning.

Starting with Ash Wednesday, Lent seemed to last forever. You had to give up something, and usually I gave up candy.* Thirty-seven candy-free, mortification-of-the-flesh days led to Good Friday, the darkest, saddest day of an already pretty dark month. There was no mass on Good Friday, but we did attend an endless three-hour service from noon until 3 p.m. where we remembered Christ's last hours on the cross. Making the fourteen stations of the cross over and over again, I always felt sad and depressed about all of our Lord's suffering, but I also wished (just a little bit) that He would hurry up and die, so we could all go home and get a break from Church and enjoy Easter Saturday before we had to trudge back into the church Sunday morning. On Easter Sunday, the church would be completely transformed again, with all the black cloths disappeared, and the Easter candle lit, and joy bells ringing, and the archbishop saying the High Mass at 10:15, wearing beautiful, embroidered pink robes and matching pink slippers, all in celebration of redemption and new beginnings and springtime, which we here in Newfoundland never get. Here on the Avalon Peninsula, April is indeed the wickedest month, bitterly cold in and out of the church. Despite the frigid temperatures, I'd be wearing my new Easter outfit, which was likely some kind of straw hat and summer coat or even a little navy blue duster.

Of course, none of these special Easter clothes had been built to withstand the icy onslaught of Newfoundland's spring. Whoever said that April's gentle breezes bring news of spring's awakening never spent an Easter morning on the steps of the

---

* On St. Patrick's Day, March 17, you were allowed to break your Lenten fast and scarf back as much candy as you could get into you for that one Lenten freebie.

Basilica of St. John the Baptist bivvering* with the cold in clothes designed for a spring that had never been known in St. John's.** They have never stood there as the wind tore in from the North Atlantic, scuttering across fields of glacial ice—wind that was fierce enough to rip the features right off your face.

I've never been able to enjoy any of the holidays or High Holy Days of Obligation. They always got me down and continue to do so to this day.

Sometimes upstairs, breaking through the ever-present quiet, Phine, Jack, and Mae would join their voices together in a full and bitter chorus of "There's no use giving anything to that crowd downstairs," or the simple, but equally contemptuous "That crowd downstairs," or a "Look what they did with the china cabinet." Oh, that china cabinet! They would not shut up about it. I can only surmise that at some point the crowd upstairs gave Mom and Dad their old china cabinet, which someone down there, probably in a drunken rage, smashed down over the stairs. Neither Aunt Phine, Uncle Jack, nor Aunt Mae ever seemed to get over that china cabinet. Any time chaos broke out downstairs, they inevitably brought up that damn cabinet, followed by a loud *tut tut tutting*, finishing off with "there's no use giving anything to that crowd," and a final, deeply disapproving "that crowd downstairs."

Being the little Benedict Arnold that I was, I would join in their disapproval and *tut tut tut* with the best of them. But that always left me in a puddle of shame. Because although I was little, I was not stund. When all of us upstairs were appalled, outraged,

---

* To shake, shiver, or tremble.

** And yet, like a crowd of meteorological morons, we waited with bated breath for a springtime that would never come.

and looking down our noses at "that crowd downstairs," even then I had an inkling that I was looking down my nose at me, too. It's very hard to say this, but I was so ashamed of the crowd downstairs, my crowd, and I was ashamed of myself, too, and so, so deeply ashamed of being ashamed. It never let up, the whispering upstairs about the awful things happening downstairs: the drinking, the fighting, the abuse, the neglect—and now, wasn't one of the sisters pregnant and only fifteen? I overheard the talk, and I hoped that my sister's pregnancy might be like Our Lady's. Maybe an angel had gotten at her? But the more I heard about it, the more I knew that my sister's pregnancy was not going to result in a glorious virgin birth, and if you believed the crowd upstairs, we might all have to die down dead with shame as a result of it. Very little escaped my shame. I was ashamed of the crowd upstairs, too. They were so old, ill, and crippled, not at all like the parents on *Leave It to Beaver* or *Father Knows Best*.

I once overheard a story that my little brother Greg had killed an old man named Muck, one of the men who used Mom and Dad's place as a party house. What I heard was that one night, Greg, who wasn't even six years old yet, was left alone in the house with Muck. The story went that Greg killed Muck by throwing a puck at him, causing him to have a heart attack. The story wasn't true. Greg never threw a puck at Muck. My brother had been playing hockey by himself down in the kitchen when all of a sudden Muck's heart gave out and poor, frightened Greg had to watch a man die on the kitchen floor in front of him. As an adult, Greg never talks about this, but I know now that he often found himself in situations that no child should have to experience alone. Yet still, despite all he went through, I was so jealous of Greg. For years I resented him intensely.

Mom and Dad loved him. They loved the sauciness of him, the speak right out and say anything to anybody-ness of him, the do what he liked and nothing else-ness of him. I mean, I could see the attraction: he was compelling. But I also thought it was outrageous because I was trying so hard to be a good little girl. Oh, I got that message early and I got it loud. *Say your prayers and brush your teeth, BE GOOD, BE GOOD, BE GOOD.* Nobody wanted trouble—except, confusingly enough, it seemed people did, because Greg was trouble with a capital "T" yet everybody loved him. It was just not fair, not fair at all as far as I could see it.

As a child I saw everything through a glass darkly. I always felt like I was on the outside looking in, no matter whether I was upstairs at number nine tut-tutting about that awful crowd downstairs, or downstairs with my parents and siblings mocking and jeering about the crowd upstairs. I didn't really belong in either place. I never felt safe downstairs, even though I longed to be down there. Being downstairs was like standing on shifting sands; I could never find my feet. Whenever I thought I was on solid ground, things inevitably took a turn for the worse. Those were always the most humiliating and embarrassing moments. They were the times I felt most lost and out of my depth. Everything that the crowd upstairs saw as good and decent was seen by the crowd downstairs as "putting on airs," "thinking too much of yourself," and "mind out now you don't swell up and bust." I didn't know how to act or how to be. And while I often wanted so badly to be downstairs, once I got there something always happened to drive me right back to the relative security of upstairs.

Downstairs was dangerous for me. I was always trying too hard, wanting to impress. I remember once when I was in about grade three, I told Mom that I'd learned all of the words to "O Canada." Mom encouraged me to stand on the stairs that led down to the kitchen and sing the whole song. I was so proud; I knew all the words; I was the star. And then, about halfway through, I looked down at my audience and realized that Mom and the rest of the family were busting a gut laughing *at* me. I was mortified. I wanted to die down dead right there on the stairs. (This was my first experience of totally misreading the room.)

Then there was the time that the ironing board was out and Mom asked me to iron a shirt. As I was doing my best, she said, "Oh my, look at her go, she can really iron! My, she's a grand girl to iron, isn't she?" I swelled up with pride, then I looked over my shoulder and saw Mom wink at my sister, and both of them were laughing at me. I think I actually burnt that shirt, not on purpose but because I was so ashamed* that I had been caught out having the nerve to think that I was something.**

At the time, I thought that everybody downstairs found me a fool, and a pompous one at that. At the time, I just wanted to fit in. Now, looking back, I consider that maybe I wasn't really trying to fit in at all: maybe I was trying to stand out. Desperately wanting to prove to my family that I was something— that I was *worth* something, and they should never have given me away in the first place. Plus, it was probably coming off me in waves: all the time I spent upstairs tut-tutting and looking down my nose at them. But at that time, I thought they were just a very mean crowd who didn't like me at all.

---

* Ashamed, the word that shows up the most whenever I revisit my childhood.
** I don't believe I ever ironed another piece of clothing.

Upstairs wasn't all that delightful either. There was the time that Uncle Jack, sitting in the captain's chair in the dining room, right next to the big window that looked out over Tank Lane, suddenly—and as far as I could see, senselessly—stood up and smashed the captain's chair through the window. He appeared to be headed out the window after the chair when Aunt Phine and Aunt Mae quickly grabbed him and held on to him for dear life. No one ever mentioned that incident again, not in my presence anyway, but Dr. O'Brien, the psychiatrist (the only one in the entire province, apparently), appeared shortly after with an ambulance to take Uncle Jack back to the Mental for another couple of months. Things got even quieter after that. Nobody said anything about Uncle Jack, but the silence was volcanic. I would be playing alone on the empty fourth floor, thinking everything was just fine when suddenly Aunt Phine would erupt in anger. Once, she smashed my favourite doll's China head to smithereens. My dolly's name was Rebecca, and she was my favourite. As well as her China head, Rebecca had China legs and a soft, squishy middle. Oh, I loved Rebecca so much, and she slept with me every night. The beauty of Rebecca was that she had a nightdress and two or three different outfits, so I could change her clothes (this was long before Barbie). Aunt Phine would often wash, starch, and iron Rebecca's best outfits. Rebecca even had a pinafore to protect her dress. Her favourite outfit was a beautiful gingham dress with a crinoline and everything.

On the day Aunt Phine smashed Rebecca's head, I was upstairs in my big empty playroom playing hospital with Rebecca and pretending she had a cut. I had somehow gotten the iodine from the medicine cabinet downstairs and was ready to treat Rebecca's imaginary cut when I spilled the whole bottle all over her freshly washed, starched, and ironed dress, soaking her outfit from the pinafore right down to the crinoline. It spread so quickly, first it was a rusty colour, then it turned purple. I watched in horror while I desperately searched in my mind for a solution to this terrible problem, but I was paralyzed. Then the door burst open and Aunt Phine charged into the room. I could tell she was already upset about something but when she saw Rebecca she flew into a Red Rage. She grabbed my dolly out of my hands, yelling words that I couldn't quite hear, because her anger had sucked all of the air out of the room and filled my head with white noise. For me, the world had slowed down and gone mute. Aunt Phine threw Rebecca with great force against the wall. Rebecca's China head exploded into shards and her beautiful blue glass eyes fell out and rolled around the floor. I sat there, frozen with shock, and then I started to cry and screech and wail. I wanted to stop crying but I couldn't. I ran out, climbed up on the banister (we had one of those old-fashioned phones set high on the wall), and called Aunt Mae at work. She promised that she would fix everything. When she came home, she was carrying a big box with a doll in it named Cynthia, who had long red hair and, mercifully, a rubber head. Once again, Aunt Mae had done just as she promised and made everything better.[*] Aunt Phine had already picked up the bits and pieces of Rebecca, including her precious glass eyes, and put them in the trash under the kitchen sink. For years, I would never look whenever I went to throw something in the garbage.

---

[*] Aunt Mae was a mother to me every day and in every way. She was soft spoken, full of kindness and compassion, and gave me so much love and care.

I was always afraid I would see one of Rebecca's beautiful blue eyes staring back at me.*

The one thing we all shared, upstairs and downstairs, was a devotion to the Blessed Virgin Mary. Nearly all the girls had Mary stuck somewhere in their name. Mom's name was Mary, Mary Johanna; Aunt Mae's was Mary Ellen. Even my oldest and toughest brother, Kevin, had such an allegiance to the Blessed Mother that he took Mary as his confirmation name. He was as brave and courageous as can be and went on to enroll in the Canadian Army. He became a champion boxer, mountain climber, and parachutist, and was never one bit ashamed of taking Our Lady's name in confirmation. And he wouldn't hesitate to put the boots to anyone who dared mock it. I, on the other hand, knew that as much as I loved Our Lady, I would, sadly, betray her in an instant.

In the sixties, the Catholics were all up in arms because the "Godless communists had taken over China." And the nuns were always warning us about the Chinese Communist Hordes who, according to the Mercy Nuns, were on the verge of invading every Christian country, including Newfoundland. The nuns made that possibility seem so real that I remember sitting in church when I was about five or six and seeing in my mind's eye hordes of Chinese communists sailing in through the Narrows, docking down at Baird's Cove and surging up over Garrison Hill. I imagined them barging in through the big red front

---

* I had a hard time with dollies. My favourite brother, Kevin, was in Germany with the Canadian Armed Forces. He sent me a full-sized walking doll. Unfortunately, the side of its head was smashed in. He was drunk when he sent it, so he didn't wrap it properly. I was still thrilled. The doll sat in pride of place in my playroom. But although I loved her, every time I walked in I was seized with surprised terror by her poor, smashed-up face, and against my will I emitted a tiny scream.

doors of the Basilica, where they would, for reasons beyond the ken of the ordinary occidental mind, desecrate the Holy Eucharist (or sacred host). And afterward, they would drive bamboo shoots underneath our little grade-oner fingernails and torture us relentlessly until we said that we did not believe in Our Lady.

Part of me really wanted to believe that maybe, for once, I'd be brave. Why couldn't I be like St. Tarcisius, one of the early Christian martyrs? Tarcisius was carrying the blessed sacrament when he was attacked by a mob and beaten to death, but he never surrendered the blessed host. I fantasized that I, too, could be just like St. Tarcisius and save the sacred host from the awful depredations of the Chinese Communist Hordes. But while I was thinking this, another part of me knew, even at the tender age of six, that as soon as I saw even one Chinese person coming toward me with anything that might vaguely resemble a bamboo shoot, I'd say "Our Lady?" laugh heartily and add "That old bag!" You see, I'd been steeping and stooping in the business of betrayal from birth, or at least since I was eight months old.

When I was growing up, and even well after, I was always afraid of everything really. Aunt Phine called me an alarmist. Much later in my life, a therapist remarked that I had had a lot to be alarmed about, and I guess I did. One day, with no prior notice to me, my family was gone. The council was tearing down the centre of the city, my neighbourhood, to make way for a shiny, new, upwardly mobile St. John's. In anticipation of this, Mom, Dad, and my siblings left 7 Carter's Hill and moved into Mom's mother's house out around the bay in Conception Harbour. I remember that as they were leaving, Aunt Phine said, "Now that I've seen the back of 'em, I don't ever want to see the front of 'em again." It had been so confusing to have my real family living next door to me. They were a daily reminder that I'd been abandoned and that I didn't belong anywhere. There's some truth to the old axiom "What the eye doesn't see, the heart doesn't feel." For a while after they were gone, everything did seem a little bit better. But then Uncle Jack died, and before Aunt Mae had an opportunity to get over that profound loss, and while she was still inconsolable, Aunt Phine had another heart attack. At first, it seemed to be the same old routine: emergency, ambulance, Father Conroy, etc. But the difference was that Aunt Phine died in the hospital. She actually died. When Aunt Mae answered the call from the hospital, they said, "Your sister has expired." Something about the way they said "expired" broke Aunt Mae's heart into a million different pieces, and she fell back in shock and gave herself quite a bad concussion. I was about eleven years old at that time and I tried really hard to feel bad about losing Aunt Phine. I knew I should feel bad, and certainly I didn't feel good, but if the truth be known I really didn't feel anything about her death. And though I was already eleven, nobody thought it was a good idea for me to go to Aunt Phine's funeral mass, and so that day I stayed home by myself in that big house on number nine.

When Aunt Mae's arthritis wasn't so bad that her knuckles were swollen up to the point where she couldn't move them, she had loved to knit. She knitted Aunt Phine a couple of beautiful sweaters that I'd always coveted: a plain beige cardigan and a sherbet-coloured sweater with a collar and matching buttons and pockets. Aunt Phine would never let me even try them on, but on the day of her funeral mass I went to Aunt Phine's highboy, took the two sweaters out of the tissue paper they were carefully wrapped in, and I wore them both all that day until I heard Aunt Mae and Dad returning home. Then I took off my favourite, the sherbet-coloured one, and put the two sweaters in my own dresser drawer. I knew in my eleven-year-old heart that it was a cold, unfeeling act to steal Aunt Phine's sweaters on the day of her burial, but obviously she didn't need them anymore.* In truth, I always felt bad about this, but now I had two new sweaters to wear to Saturday roller-skating at the stadium instead of the same tired red turtleneck I wore every week. So I felt good about the new sweaters and terribly guilty and ashamed about them, too.

When Aunt Phine died, Aunt Mae was absolutely destroyed. Without Uncle Jack and Aunt Phine in her life, she was alone and bereft, left to look after me all by herself. Most days she just couldn't see her way forward. Dad had come out to town from around the bay for Aunt Phine's funeral, and on the day she was buried, I overheard him say to Aunt Mae that it was time for me to move back in with the family, that she couldn't look after me anymore; I was too much for her. Although I heard this conversation, it was like I didn't. Or maybe I thought the conversation was about a different little girl, because I know I did not say to Aunt Mae, "No, don't let me go," or "Yes, please let me go if

---

* This reminds me of the incident during the winter I was in grade two when one of my classmates slid down Garrison Hill on her bookbag, right under the wheels of an oncoming truck. The wake was at her home on Duckworth Street. The whole class was there, and I felt terribly sad until I saw the nun doll in her casket. I had wanted a nun doll badly but seemed to be cursed to never get one. And I remember thinking, "That's just a waste of a perfectly good nun doll." Of course, if I'd been any more of a heartless sociopath, I would have reached into her coffin and snatched the doll when no one was looking. Thanks be to God, I didn't go that far.

they really want me." I said nothing. I knew it wasn't that my family really wanted me; Dad just thought I was a handful and too much for a crippled old aunt who was now all on her own.

I don't know how it happened because I was so desperately trying to not pay attention to anything at the time, but Dad went back around the bay without me. I was safe with Aunt Mae—for the time being anyway. When she was still alive, Aunt Phine would often remark that maybe I'd be "better off with my own kind." She'd go on to mutter under her breath that God alone knew that she and Mae would be a lot better off without all the torment. When Aunt Phine said that, Aunt Mae would smile at me reassuringly and I'd feel better. But each time Aunt Phine said something similar, I'd feel my heart rise up in my throat and I'd know just how tenuous my situation was. "If not here, then where?" I'd think. I'd soon find out.

After Aunt Phine's death, there were so many changes. I was changing, going through that horrible puberty stage with my hormones up on bust. I had no idea where I stopped and the world began, and all around me my world was crumbling. I was angry with Aunt Mae for being so devastated and so sad. I didn't want to be angry, but I couldn't help it. I needed her to be Aunt Mae. I needed her to be the rock she'd always been in my life, so I just didn't want to see or in any way acknowledge her despair. For about a year or so I could barely look at Aunt Mae. It was hard work ignoring her deep unhappiness, but I was determined to do just that. Some part of me felt, or perhaps knew, that I wasn't strong enough to take on her deep unhappiness.

Even before the city took the house on Carter's Hill, Aunt Mae had sold everything: her rosewood Victrola, the heavy mahogany table and dining room set, the big stuffed whitecoat seal that used to take pride of place in front of the hearth in the dining room, all of our furniture from number nine except the beds. We already had no living room furniture, because all that had been sold when Uncle Jack first got sick. He needed to sleep downstairs so he wouldn't have to face another steep flight of stairs. But now it was all gone.

Aunt Mae bought a house on Rankin Street in Rabbittown, which was not downtown at least. I was thrilled to have a house with a yard. It wasn't in around the back of town, where I really wanted to be, but it was still a step up from our previous home. Unlike the rest of my family, I was a shameless social climber. I desperately wanted to live on one of the tree streets with all the people from the middle class, not deep in the downtown surrounded by the hoi polloi (in fact, my people). Downtown all the houses were glommed together one on top of the other, and I realized that at that time in St. John's, this was how you lived if you were poor. The crowd that had money, on the other hand, the good crowd, the crowd I aspired to be part of, had space. They had a yard around the house and room to breathe without having to breathe in your neighbours' breath.

Our new house was totally empty, and there was depressing brown fake panelling on the walls of every room, including the kitchen. Aunt Mae found the panelling particularly distressing, and because she was grieving, she didn't have the energy or the inclination to go about furnishing this sad and empty house, a house she in fact hated. I could see how Aunt Mae felt about it, but in my scramble to rise ever upward, I saw the house as a step in the right direction.

I did everything I could to bully, manipulate, or convince Aunt Mae to stop being unhappy and start accepting our new home. I tried to cook something every day after school so there would be food ready when she got home after work. It was grim; I was a terrible cook. After supper, I tried to keep up a good face, but most nights I locked myself in my room, claiming I was studying. In reality, I was hiding away from Aunt Mae's raw and awful grief. After a while it became too much even for me. My joy at finally getting out of downtown and having a yard couldn't stand up against the reality of the house. It was always dark. It seemed to be forever November in that house, with the night closing in and the darkness swallowing everything even before I managed to get home from school. I could feel myself getting worn down by the darkness of the house and the unhappiness of Aunt Mae. It was hard to ignore both, but I remained determined to do just that.

Every Saturday, Aunt Mae went to confession. I went with her and waited on the pew outside the confessional for my turn. Sometimes Aunt Mae took forever in there with the priest, and on those days I knew she was talking about me. I knew it because she told me so. She'd always felt that she wasn't quite up to the job of raising me alone. Often she'd say to me, "Here I am with neither chick nor child," and I would think, "What about me?" Then she'd add, "If I was your real mother, maybe I'd know better what to do." Aunt Mae didn't know how to do it all on her own, so she sought advice from the place where she always went for help: the Church.

One Saturday, after she had been in the confessional for what seemed like an endless amount of time, Aunt Mae came out and declared she couldn't live one more minute on Rankin Street. She told me she was going to sell the house and that she and I were moving to Cherry Hill Road. The plan was for us to board with Uncle Jack's old friend and his wife. The man used to come to watch *Hockey Night in Canada* with Uncle Jack every Saturday night. My heart sank. That man had never liked me, even when I was at that cute "everybody loves a little girl with big fat cheeks and thick brown plaits tied up with satin bows" stage. I knew I was now an awkward and potentially deeply unlikable adolescent, but there was nothing for it. Aunt Mae said that she and I were going to share a room because that's all the space the couple had, and they were only taking us in out of the goodness of their hearts. We would have to do our best to keep out of the way and eat everything that was put in front of us.

Aunt Mae said this was a godsend for her because she couldn't go on for much longer with just the two of us living in that awful dark house. She opened up to me about her despair around the loss of first Uncle Jack, and then Aunt Phine, who had always looked after her. I knew she was opening her heart, but I just couldn't listen; it was too much. I started to get a sinking feeling that I, too, was part of the overall awfulness of Aunt Mae's new life.

Of late I've come to the astounding conclusion that I was depressed when I was young. I had childhood depression, if a child can be diagnosed with that condition. I don't remember much of my childhood, but I do remember heading off to Mercy Convent from our house on 9 Carter's Hill and looking back at our wooden storm door, painted that traditional St. John's oxblood red, and just feeling so sad. A kind of nameless, swirling sadness. Then I would turn around and trudge my way off to school for another day with the nuns.* I tried so hard to put a good face on it, to be chirpy and lighthearted (this attitude in and of itself must have seemed totally phony and would have irritated my real family beyond belief).

Upstairs depression.

Downstairs liquor and chaos.

And for a long time, I lived with depression.

---

* Actually, the nuns were always nice to me during those early years. They liked me because I was precocious and so grown up.

M*om*

I WAS ALWAYS SO MAD AT MOM. TO MY MIND EVERY-thing about her was wrong. I hated her and the way she was, although I never let on to her that I felt that way because I was so terrified of her. She was a large, imposing woman with a will of iron. You knew that if she told you to do something and you didn't do it, she would go through brick walls to get at you, haul you back by the hair of your head and, if she had to, she was ready to crucify you all day long until you obeyed her orders. Our nickname for her was "The Sarge," for very good reason.

One night when I was about eleven or twelve, after the whole family had moved up to Conception Harbour, my sisters (who for many complex reasons were back home living with my mother) were grown women with children of their own. Mom had warned them not to go out and leave the youngsters at home by themselves. When Mom got home after a party, she found that Lol (Laura) and Donna (Madonna), my two older sisters, had seen their chance and taken off. Somehow, she got the news that they were jarred up over in a party house in Avondale, drinking. Mom summoned Willy Whalen, the Conception Bay Central taximan, shoved all of my sisters' seven youngsters in the back of the taxi, and sped over to Avondale. When she arrived at the party house, she threw a brick through the window, kicked in the door, and shoved the children inside, yelling something along the lines of "Look after your youngsters, you bloods of bitches!"

Another time, Mom promised my fifteen-year-old brother Frank (a great dancer who could jive like nobody's business) that if he scrubbed all the floors downstairs she would give him a dollar to go to the dance in Colliers. But after he'd scrubbed said floors, Mom laughed at him, refused to give him the dollar, and told him he wasn't allowed to go to the dance. Since she was cunning and all-knowing, and recognizing his passion for dancing, she had taken the precaution of hiding his shoes. Frank, still desperate to go, found an old pair of hockey skates. He threw them out of his second-story bedroom window, somehow shimmied down from there, put on the skates, and hobbled out the road until he got to a friend's house, where he borrowed some shoes and triumphantly went off to Colliers to dance his heart out at the parish hall. He thought he was home free—but not so fast. Mom once again called Willy Whalen, who drove her to Colliers, where she burst into the dance and strode over to Frank, grabbed him by the ear, and much to his humiliation, hauled him out of there. The story goes that Frank didn't even say anything beyond whispering, "Mom, you're some mean." And as if all this wasn't enough evidence of the Power of Mom, the priest in Conception Harbour, speaking from the pulpit that Sunday morning, repeated the story, praising Mom's superior mothering techniques, and exhorted the other mothers to behave more like her. Frank's humiliation was complete.*

Mom was terrifying, but people loved her, and of course the truth was that I did, too. I longed for her to look at me and say, "I'm so sorry we gave you away, darling; can you ever forgive me?" To which, for most of my life, I would have answered a resounding "NO." I still don't understand why they did it, and mostly I blamed Mom.

ONCE WHEN I WAS IN ARIZONA, I ATTENDED A SESSION called family constellation therapy. I had no understanding of what the therapy entailed. When I arrived, a group of people was already there, and I thought, "Oh okay, group therapy, that might be helpful." But as it turned out, these people were there to take on the roles of my various family members, acting out the dynamics of all my childhood wounds. My therapist, as part of the group, had related some of my story. I was mortified. I thought it was the most ridiculous thing I'd ever taken part in. One member played Mom, another played Dad, and someone else was me at eight months old. There was even someone playing my lungs.

As the session went forward, I became less and less embarrassed and more and more emotionally involved, until, at the end, the two perfect strangers who were playing my mother and father looked a sobbing me in the eyes and said the words I'd always hoped my parents would say to me: "We love you

---

* When my brother tells this story, he always adds that Mom's great rival, Annie Mae, did the same thing to her two sons at a dance in Colliers the following week. To Mom's delight, the priest didn't even mention it from the pulpit.

very much. We were totally wrong to have ever given you away. Can you forgive us?" To which, still sobbing, I blurted out: "I forgive him, but I will never ever, ever forgive her!"

It was an interesting afternoon.

MOM WAS SO FUNNY. A LOT OF HER HUMOUR WAS SARcasm; she was devastatingly sarcastic. The word is from the Greek *sarkazein*, which means "to tear flesh." And boy, could Mom ever strip you to the bone with a few well-chosen words! Yet she was the life of every party. She loved to dance and sing. She never missed a wake or a wedding, or any sort of gathering at all, or really, any place where people got together to drink and carouse, laugh and enjoy themselves.* Whenever she'd get a few drinks in, she'd sing, "The red red robin goes bob bob bobbin along" or that Neil Diamond song "Red, Red Wine." She loved red. When I later played Nancy Reagan in a skit on the Codco show I wore a red dress, and she said it was the best she'd ever seen me look.

When my family was still living next door at 7 Carter's Hill,** out of the blue, she unexpectedly gave me a spring coat for my birthday. I somewhat dimly recall that it was red. Red for anger, they say. And she was often angry. Now, when I see her in my mind's eye being explosively angry and terrifying the entire house, I can see that she was also full of fear. Much later in life, I realized that Mom was fearful of many, many things, but when I was young I could only think of

---

* It runs right through our whole family; we appear so kind and generous to strangers yet we treat the people we're closest to very differently indeed.

** See "The Little Girl Who Grew Up Next Door to Her Family."

how afraid of her I was. So were we all. She did like some of her youngsters, but only the ones who stood up to her and sauced her back. She never took to the timid or the panicky ones, and I was definitely one of those, particularly when I was around her.

Though I resented Mom bitterly, I was aching for her love. I know now that the reason I was so mad at her and resented her so much and for so long was because I so desperately needed her attention, acceptance, and love. I knew Aunt Mae loved me, but hers wasn't the love I wanted.*

After the family had moved up to Conception Harbour, I'd stay with them in the summer off a week or two. When we got home from Sunday mass on those bright, sunny summer days, there'd be about an hour before we all sat down and dug into the big boilers full of vegetables and pans of meat and gravy. *Oh God*, Mom's gravy. Just the smell of that dinner could fill you up, it was so good. And there'd be dessert. Sometimes she'd make a Duncan Hines chocolate cake iced with Cadbury milk chocolate bars. But instead of being delighted to have a cake iced with chocolate bars, I was filled with resentment. "Not even a real cake, just a cake mix," I thought, "with just chocolate bars on the top. That's the best she can do?" I loved her so much and needed so much from her, and I felt I got so little, it made me bitter and angry. I was always furious with her. Why I felt that my rage would ever get me what I so desperately wanted from her, her love and attention, I have no idea. This year I am seventy-two, the same age my mother was when she died, and

---

* The beginning of a lifelong pattern of never wanting what I had and always longing for what I didn't have.

finally, bit by bit, I'm letting go. They say that to understand is to forgive, and so . . .

My mom was born in Conception Harbour,* in September 1914, just one month after the start of the Great War. She grew up in a time of faeries and boo-darbies. A time when angels were commonplace, and spirits, miracles, and magic, both dark and white, all existed. These things were all a part of my mother's everyday life.** Her grandfather had "the gift" of second sight. Once in the midst of a raging storm, sailing down to the Labrador, a terrified crewmate grabbed my great-grandfather by the arm and begged him, "Bless the waves and make them go back!" To which he replied, "Bless them yourself, you goddamn Protestant!" If someone drowned while they were fishing down on the Labrador, word would not come back to their family for months, but my great-grandfather would know it the day of the loss. He would dream that night of the drowned man walking up through the gap in his fence, and my great-grandfather would say that he could hear the water squelching in the poor dead man's rubber boots.

My mother's own mother walked in the ditch every All Souls' Night, the night after Halloween. She didn't want to disturb the dead souls who were up out of their graves and walking on the road. Grandmom would always leave bread on her babies' faces if she had to go outside to check the

---

* Conception Harbour includes the former communities of Bacon Cove, Cat's Cove, Kitchuses, and Silver Spring. It has a history of fishing, whaling, and ironworking industries. It has ties to the steel-working and construction industry starting at the turn of the twentieth century in the eastern United States.

** Life for my mom was like in a Gabriel García Márquez novel. What was commonplace was seen as magical, and what was miraculous was thought to be common.

clothesline or haul water. The bread was to fool the faeries,* so they'd take it and not the baby. Faeries were rampant in those days, and always on the lookout for babies to steal or for people to lead astray into faerieland. My mother was often faerie-led when she picked blueberries, but she knew enough to simply turn her apron and bring herself back to this dimension.

With all this whimsical talk of faeries and otherworldly magic it might sound as if Mom's crowd were a sweet, fanciful family, innocent and naïve, with a deep belief in the supernatural and perhaps a very loose grip on reality. In fact, according to the stories that have come down through the generations, they were always a hard-nosed, hard drinking, often cruel crowd, almost brutal, who liked nothing as much as humiliating and demeaning each other under the guise of helping the other person become someone who could both dish it out and also take it. I imagine they thought they were arming each other so they'd be better equipped to face a harsh, grim, and grievous world. And for many people, including Mom's family, that is an accurate picture of the world.

After the failure of the fishery in the 1920s, work became non-existent. Like many other people in the area, Mom's father went to New York to work high steel. He did not come home for many years. Ironworkers, because of the risk and the brutal nature of their work, made $17 a week, an unheard-of sum then for labourers. For years and years, Grandfather didn't send a penny home to his wife and six children. Grandmom

---

* Faerie: A small imaginary being of human form that has magical powers, especially a female one. Definition from Oxford Languages.

and her children were reduced, according to an old boyfriend of Mom's, to eating grass.

Mom's father, when he finally did return, was by all accounts a hard man. There is a story that Mom's baby brother, my uncle George, fell through the ice on Healey's Pond. And though he saw his father walk in the road, he was so afraid of him that he felt it better to freeze and drown rather than risk his father's wrath. Once Mom's sister Aunt Laura ate a whole lit cigarette rather than let her father catch her smoking. They say that Mom's mother, Christine, was a religious fanatic who was so affected by years of near starvation that she would keep food until it went bad for fear there would be nothing to replace it. Finally, when the chicken, or whatever it was, went green, she would cook it up and serve it to her children.

At a very young age, Mom and her sister Cass were forced to go into service in St. John's, where they worked long hours for nothing but room and board. On lots of British shows, like *Upstairs Downstairs* and *Downton Abbey*, the working poor, in service to the upper classes, seem to lavish a lot of love and adoration on their employers. This certainly wasn't the case for Mom and Aunt Cass. They worked under harsh conditions and were treated abominably, and for the most part they resented and deeply disliked their employers and were begrudging of the work they were forced to do. Aunt Cass, who was in service to a particularly brutal family out on Kenmount Road, was angry most of the time. She ended up taking out some of her bitterness on the children of the house. According to Mom, when they were mocking her sister, jeering at her, and calling her a "stupid old bay noddy maid,"

Aunt Cass would chase them. "Oh, Cass," Mom would say, "She wouldn't go after them youngsters with just her hands. Oh no, it was always a knife or scissors she would chase after them with."

When she was sixteen, Mom went to work for a woman whose husband was a captain on a ship. The woman had an unnaturally close and loving relationship with her stove: she wanted it to be shiny and clean enough that she could see her face reflected in it. Consequently, whenever her husband was at sea, she refused to light the stove. So Mom was starved the whole time she worked there, "her stomach thought her throat was cut," and she was reduced to eating crackers and bread and anything else that didn't need to be cooked. Mom was always hungry.* Even when I was a teenager, she could still eat a gallon of potatoes and a full pan of fat and salt fish. My brother Frank always said, "It's a good thing our mother was hungry, or else we probably would have all starved to death."

One year, desperate for work, Mom signed on to cook and look after a crew of men prosecuting the Labrador Fishery. Down on the Labrador the men outnumbered the women five to one, with the men traditionally starting to work around age twelve and the women as young as eleven. Mom was young when she arrived and quite literally grew up working on the Labrador. They say the women on the Labrador worked like Torbay ponies:** from stars-in-the-sky morning till stars-in-the-sky

---

* "Hungry for life, hungry for love, hungry for donuts, hungry for anything that isn't nailed down." A quote from Codco's "Bernie Snelgrove: Superstar."

** Torbay ponies were known for their strength and resilience, which stemmed from the harsh environment they lived in and the demands of their work.

night. They cooked, cleaned, made the fish, and spread it on the bawn,* tended whatever gardens there were, knit, spun wool, picked berries, washed, and sewed. Once when I was about twelve, I walked into the front room to find Mom weeping as she watched a local television show, *Land and Sea*. It was the first time I'd ever seen my mother cry, and probably the last. The episode was devoted to the Labrador Fishery, and Mom was crying because down on the Labrador was the best time she ever had in her whole life. She spoke with great feeling of places called Cut Throat, Splittin' Knife, and Black Tickle. She remembered, with tears in her eyes, the grand dances they had at the whaling factory in Graedy, telling me, "The smell would suffocate you, but oh the fun!"

Depending on the weather and the ice conditions, the fishery work could begin in May and end in November; the average voyage lasted from early June until late September. I don't know if Mom travelled down to the Labrador on a schooner, where she'd have had to sleep on piles of fishing twine for the journey, or on a steamer, where the women and girls had bunks. They were all in close quarters, and people who, under normal circumstances, might be separated by religion, class, and gender had to pull together for the good of all.

According to Clara Joan Doyle Murphy Rutherford** and her thesis "The Place of the Labrador Fishery in the Folklife of a Newfoundland Community," social norms started to loosen up as soon as the boats crossed the Strait of Belle Isle. Even

---

* An expanse of rocks on which salted cod is spread for the quick-drying process of the Labrador and Banks Fisheries; BEACH.
** Oh, pick a name.

before they arrived at the fishing stations, some of the men crawled in the bunks with the women and it's reported that the women had to throw salt in their eyes to get rid of them. But once they hit the fishing stations on the Labrador, many of the moral confines and restrictions that were firmly held in community were simply thrown away. Something called *gulching* was common on Cut Throat Island, the northeastern island where the people of Mom's community had their fishing stations. In the dictionary of Newfoundland English, *gulch* is defined as frequenting a sheltered hollow for sexual intimacy. Doyle Rutherford cites the earliest description of gulching from the *Journal of American Folklore* in 1895: "Gulch has come, on the Labrador coast, to have a meaning peculiar to that region and to these who frequent it. In the summer, men, women, and children from Newfoundland spend some weeks there at the fishing, living in a very promiscuous way. As there is no tree for shelter for hundreds of miles of islands and shores, parties resort to the hollows for secret indulgence. Hence gulching has, among them, become a synonym for living a wanton life."

Mom lived a very hard life working night and day just to survive, and so who would deny her a bit of wantonness? Well, me I guess. I was shocked at how openly sexual and ardently flirtatious Mom would be with any fella, young or old. When I and Cathy Jones, a colleague from Codco, visited Mom with Cathy's then-boyfriend, Marvin, the first thing Mom said to Cathy, looking hard at Marvin, was "Is he any good in the bed?" A friend from Mom's youth would often visit the house, and my father, if he was drinking, would became rageful and jealous and challenge Mom's "friend" to step outside to fight him. It seemed so ridiculous that Dad could still be jealous of that huge mound of Mom flesh, but we found out later that in fact, Mom and her friend were still "goin' at it," sometimes right on the couch in the front room.

Mom met my father in 1937 while she was again down working on the Labrador.* Dad was an engineer on the steamer *Imongen*, which picked up salt fish from the fishing stations in an attempt to get it to the European markets faster than the competition. He fell in love with Mom, and from what I can remember, stayed in love with her for the next forty or so years they were together. He loved her, but I'm not sure she ever felt very much for him.** He was thirty-nine years old, a veteran of the First World War, and an inveterate sailor. Mom was twenty-three, and maybe it was her wantonness that captured him. Dad wanted Mom to marry him. Mom definitely didn't want to marry Dad. She referred to him contemptuously as the "old fella." Mom had much bigger plans for herself.

Mom wanted to get into the States, and it should have been easy for her because most of her brothers and sisters were already down there and she could have been sponsored in. She wanted to get to New York so badly; most of her close friends from Conception Harbour had already emigrated down there.

---

* Much later, when I was visiting my dad at his nursing home in Holyrood, an old man came up to me and said, "You're Pol D's daughter aren't you?" (Pol was short for Polly, Polly at one time was a common enough nickname for Mary, and D was for Dalton, Mom's maiden name.) When I told him I was, he said, "One time down on the Labrador I put a rat right down her bosom. Well, she got such a fright that she jumped right overboard into the icy Labrador Sea."

** When Mom was around, Dad never really let on how much he loved her. It was only when she was away that he'd sing her praises endlessly; if they were in the same room, there seemed to be no love lost between them.

"It was like dying and going to heaven," Norah Gull, one of Mom's friends, said about moving to New York in the thirties. "They treated us like we were human beings."

The men from Mom's hometown were going up there to New York to work high steel, "making the biggest kinda money," and all of Mom's sisters and most of her friends went up as biddies or maids until they got on their feet. Newfoundland was its own country at the time, and so we had an American embassy in St. John's. When Mom applied to go to the States, she had to have a physical. The doctor at the embassy (who Mom forevermore called "that bastard doctor") said Mom had tuberculosis; he turned down her application to emigrate three times. In despair, Mom married "the old fella," my dad. How could Dad ever compete with the great American dream promised to anyone who moved to the Land of the Free and the Home of the Brave?

They married in 1938, and by September 1939 my brother Kevin was born. Kevin was so handsome. He looked just like Dad had looked when he was young, a matinee idol. By 1947, Mom and Dad were legally separated, and Dad had sole custody of their four children: Kevin, Michael, Madonna, and Laura. I was born in 1952, after they got back together, and sometimes when Dad had a few drinks in him he'd say that he was sure I was his. What happened between 1946 and 1952 is deeply murky and hidden and will remain so for the purposes of this essay.* No one in the family besides me ever wants to talk about it. Eventually, Mom and Dad got back together, had a dead baby (Baby Walsh), then me, and then my little brother, Greg. And

---

* They're a tough crowd, my family, and I don't want them coming after me.

for reasons beyond the ken of an ordinary child's mind, they decided to give me away.

Recently I read a fascinating article in the *London Review of Books* called "Mothers Were Different." It was a review written by Susan Pedersen of a book named *Bread Winner: An Intimate History of the Victorian Economy* by Emma Griffin. As I read it, I realized that my family was a perfect Victorian working-class family; we just lived in the wrong century. The book itself was a history of nineteenth-century working-class families, mostly dock workers, in East London. It described London's working-class mothers and how their love was never expressed with caresses. The good mother in the Victorian working class might hit her children, shout at them, show no interest in their imagination or development, or even any interest in them at all, but she kept food in their bellies and coats on their backs. And really, that was as much as she could manage in her sixteen-hour workday.

We think now that parents, especially mothers, should nurture their children, but mothers in the nineteenth century had no time to nurture. They had more than enough to do just to keep their children alive. Fathers were the single providers,* and many women and children of the Victorian era had the misfortune to be dependent on bad providers, men who could have supported their families but spent their money on their own pleasures instead. My family was fortunate that our dad was, in Victorian terms, a good provider. Victorian children were well aware and grateful that a good father was a good provider. They witnessed, as we did, the weekly ritual of their father

---

* It was the same in my family, since Mom could not be in service or work on a boat down on the Labrador when she had a house full of youngsters.

turning over his pay packet, unopened, to his wife. In Victorian times, a good father didn't have to be interested in his children or especially like them. He merely had to accept that they were his responsibility.

In Victorian working-class terms, Mom was an excellent mother. She fulfilled all those obligations. Dad was a great father because every week without fail, he turned over his pay packet to Mom. There is a story that once, when Dad was three or four sheets to the wind, he rolled in and handed Mom his pay packet as usual but made the mistake of foolishly getting my brother Greg's attention, pointing to his cap and winking. Greg immediately tattled to Mom, who knocked Dad's cap off his head and found his hidden overtime pay. Any of us would have turned Dad in the same way Greg did. As children, we were on Mom's side. She had all the power, and she seemed to hold our father in deep contempt. She wanted nothing to do with him, and to our great shame, we acted as if we felt that way, too, although we never did.

Reading that article in the *London Review of Books* made me reconsider everything I felt about Mom. It made me wonder if her life, and the hard-bitten and sometimes cruel way she behaved was (just as in Victorian working-class England) structural and inescapable. I had always blamed her and her personality for my unhappiness. When I lived upstairs with my aunt Mae and my aunt Phine, they would often remark—when things got particularly noisy and chaotic in my parents' house downstairs—"Your mother married your father for a meal ticket." I felt so ashamed of that. But I think now that just as Jane Austen wrote in *Pride and Prejudice*, "Marriage is the only honourable provision for women of small fortune and their pleasantest preservative from want." For many working class women in the Victorian era, and certainly for my Mom, marriage seemed to provide the ONLY preservative from want.*

They were careless, Mom and Dad. They drank too much and partied too hard, and because their house was always open to anyone who had a case of beer or a bottle of whiskey, my brothers and sisters were often left unprotected and unlooked-after.**

The recent realization that later shocked me was that though consciously I was angry with Mom, subconsciously I had emulated her in every way possible. I took in and embraced all of Mom's beliefs and loves and prejudices. I wanted everything she wanted. I was like a sponge, soaking up all of Mom. It was like if I couldn't HAVE her, I could BE her. I didn't become aware of any of this until I was in my mid-sixties. Of course, many of Mom's beliefs were just plain wrong. What Mom admired was not necessarily admirable, and what she embraced I had to eventually learn to let go of. I had a blind devotion to Mom, while at the same time I was filled with anger and resentment toward her.

---

* Jane Austen also said that single women have a dreadful propensity for being poor, which is one very strong argument in favour of matrimony.

** Just this year, I was visiting my brother Michael in the hospital. I always felt a little intimidated by him. I was sitting by his bed when he looked over at me and said, "It's my fault they gave you away." No one up to that point, except for my sister Lol, had ever said anything about my being given away. I truly felt that no one in my family had ever thought about it, or cared. Mike went on to say, "The Old Woman [that's what he always called Mom] went out and told me to keep the fire goin', but I was playin' cards and never thought about it. That's when you got pneumonia. My fault. I know it's been hard on you." I'm still stunned and immensely moved by the fact that I did exist in my family's thoughts all those years, and that Mike had felt guilty, needlessly guilty. He was only eleven years old at the time, too young to be left in charge of a baby and a wood stove. More proof of parental neglect and general carelessness.

But luckily, those days are long past. Because I grew up on the outside of my family, I had no understanding of family or what being in a real family meant. Until I was over seventy years old, I didn't really comprehend or appreciate what my family's familial style was. I couldn't see past all the fighting and the blows and the low, mean remarks to recognize how kind and how caring the people in my family were to one another.

As Greg was calling his brother "the biggest kind of big fat cunt," he was also busy helping that sick and frail brother into the shower. I didn't understand that for all of the outward toughness and hard-man fronts they put on, the women as much as the men—we were trying to be "as big a man as Mom was"—how deeply they cared. When I'd recently given up smoking and drinking, and had just broken up with my son's father—and was incapable of doing much beyond throwing myself to the floor in a flurry of sobs, though I still had a toddler to look after—my sister Lol flew in to the rescue. She saved us on so many occasions. But it wasn't just Lol, it was all of them. My sister Carol rushed home from thousands of miles across the country to provide daily help to my brother Frank when his wife was suddenly struck down with illness.

I realized then that my siblings must have learned some, if not all, of this ability to love and care for each other from someone. Maybe it was Mom.

Carter's Hill

AT THE TOP OF THE BOTTOM PART OF CARTER'S HILL there was a lion's head cistern where the really poor people in our neighbourhood went with buckets and pumped water out of the big lion's mouth. I loved that water cistern. We played there all the time, and I was always secretly glad that at 9 Carter's Hill we had water right in the house. Having water also meant that we didn't have to wait for the night soil truck to come around and pick up what we could so easily just flush away. And though we played there all the time, I was always secretly a little bit ashamed of my neighbourhood, but I loved it anyway.

By the time I was eleven, the house on Carter's Hill was taken by City Council. All the downtown core of the city was going to be torn down in a big act of Municipal Magical Thinking. It was '60s social engineering at its very worst: the idea that if you tore down the housing of the poor, therefore getting rid of where the poor lived, you could somehow get rid of the poor. My grade six teacher, Sister Mary Bernadette, told us that she actually wept with happiness when she heard that my house and my neighbourhood were going to be destroyed. Sister Mary Bernadette had a long thin aquiline nose, which she used to great effect to look down with pity and contempt on the girls who were poor in our class. She said she'd been praying to Jesus that a fire would rage over that part of St. John's, burn it to the ground, and get rid of it forever.

I was taken aback by Sister Bernadette's passionate response to the destruction of my home. But in a way I, too, was happy to get out of there. I was always embarrassed to live downtown rather than In Around the Back of Town where the "in" girls lived, the girls who had the dad with the big job, and the mom and the little brothers and sisters, and the car, and a house in on a tree street, Pinebud or Maple, the kind of *Father Knows Best* family from TV. Or like David and Anne's crowd (the Catholic version of Dick and Jane) from the grade one reader. I imagined they lived in good, decent, Catholic kinds of families, where Father gave Mother a statue of the Blessed Virgin as a birthday present.*

After the council took our house, Aunt Mae and I had to move, not exactly in around the back of town where the rich girls lived, but at least up out of downtown. And while I was busy being happy about that, while my back was turned, the city council tore out the whole centre of St. John's. They got rid of the warm, beating heart of the old city, the oldest city in North America. It was never to be replaced. My dad, a dyed-in-the-wool Townie born in 1898, always said that St. John's was a city when New York was a mud hole. Dad said that once upon a

---

* I always thought that if I was Mother, I would be very, very disappointed in that present.

time almost everyone in the middle of St. John's worked down on the harbour, probably Longshore, but now the Longshore union membership was dwindling and machines were offloading cargo. But things were very different, he said, in the old days. In the old days, the centre of St. John's would be alive with men going down to the harbour at six in the morning, and you could watch them come home, walking up over the hillsides, for a second breakfast at nine o'clock. You could see them if you were up on Long's Hill, or Cabot Street, or even up high on Carter's Hill: a wave of working men whose back-breaking labour made a second breakfast an absolute necessity.

But now they were tearing out all that part of St. John's. It was the beginning of the end of the whole neighbourhood. The end of seeing the Holy Man every day. The Holy Man was small and painfully thin, with thick glasses and some sort of shaking disorder. His right hand always held his left across his front and the left hand always shook. He lived in a green house across from us on Tank Lane. Alone? I never knew. I only saw him when he was at the Basilica, or on his way back and forth to the Basilica. No matter what corner of the church I came around, there he was, the Holy Man. It was goodbye to Mr. Coady, who had a forge with a big open roaring fire. His forge looked just like something from one of those Saturday morning Westerns. In the winter, Mr. Coady would always let me and my brother come in out of the cold whenever we spent the afternoon sliding down the big hill behind our house. Years later, I can still smell Mr. Coady's forge. It had an acrid, smoky, kind of irony smell. Sometimes Mr. Coady would give me and my little brother five cents because he knew our dad from working with him down on the Longshore. Now there'd be no more playing with Boopy and Tishy Breen, my best friends. I'd miss Boopy and Tishy, but they had already moved on to somewhere in Ontario, I think.

What I knew I wouldn't miss was the sight of the Scary Man running down Carter's Hill from Tessier Place with the blood running down his face. I only saw him once when I was very young, but the image stayed with me forever. After that, every time I looked through the second-floor window I could always see him running, see the blood, see his terror, and feel it right in the very centre of myself.

There'd be no more playing cowboys and Indians or Russians and Americans in Laundry Lane, the perfect place to play those games. Gone, too, were the beautiful houses in the garden, where Geraldine Mullins and her brother Tommy ("who worked for the Priestesses") and sometimes her sister Kathleen (when she was drinking, it would take at least six policemen to get Kathleen into the back of the Black Maria) lived. We wouldn't be going to O'Keefe's grocery, where they had the huge round of hard cheese and the vats of salt meat and riblets. No more Ruby's store next to Nick's Snack Bar, and the Bay buses would have to park somewhere else, so we'd never again see Mrs. Ruby holding a fried egg up to the bare lightbulb to check if there really was a blood spot in the yolk, and if she would have to return the money (back then people could buy eggs, not just cigarettes, *by the each*). And no more Burke's Square, or Brazil Square, or Pinky Lane, or James Lane, or Lions Square, or Finn Street. No more white-as-a-ghost, totally bald, tall tall thin John D. Snow and his store, piled from floor to ceiling with books and milk bottles and odd bits of glass and old overcoats. Millions and millions and millions of dusty, ill-used old paperbacks, and Mr. Snow, never smiling, and standing there, the king of his empire of junk. And Sidel's Store was gone; and Mr. Sidel's brother the tailor down at the bottom of Bates Hill; and Crotty's Taxi; and Boopy crying that Mr. Crotty killed my little brother Greg, but not really, he just knocked him down. And the Chinese club on Bates Hill, where they said Chinese men went to play cards and gamble, was gone. Mammy Gosse's, the Ritz Tavern, and Dynamite Dunn's—all gone. There was no one left now to say "Come up to the top of Casey Street till I beats the bake off ya." No more of those hard hard R's, no more long A's. A whole vibrant, dynamic culture of people and their definitive downtown, working-class, Townie sound, gone.

And no more sisters and brothers, and mother and father for me to live next door to. Before Aunt Mae and I moved out of number nine, Mom and Dad had already moved up to Conception Harbour up around the bay, to Mom's mother's house in on The Pinch, and so, just like that, I would never be the Little Girl Growing Up Next Door to My Family ever again.

Come Home Year

IT'S 1966, NEWFOUNDLAND'S FIRST EVER COME HOME Year, and the provincial government is encouraging Newfoundlanders from all over to come home and enjoy the warmth of an Old World welcome in the New Newfoundland. Since 1949, when we somewhat-against-the-will of at least 49 percent of the population, joined the Confederation of Canada, Joey Smallwood, Newfoundland's premier and Father of Confederation, had been busy hauling Newfoundland and Newfoundlanders, kicking and screaming, out of a nineteenth-century economy into the industrialized twentieth century. Now, Joey was inviting all the Newfoundland expatriates and even some of our new Canadian brethren to come and see the progress we had so proudly made over the last seventeen years. Everyone was invited to gaze in awe at the 1,800 miles of new roads, to watch more and better hospitals being built, to see how centuries of isolation were being brought to an end.

"Just look at the hockey stick factory in Stephenville," we said.

"The shoe manufacturer in Harbour Grace."

"The rubber tire plant in Holyrood."

"And how about that chocolate factory in Carbonear, particularly that delicious orange flavour?"

Newfoundland was busily building for her future. Building a Province of Progress and Promise. And we wanted everyone to come home and celebrate with us and see how far we'd come. It was a time of great hope and potential. But not, however, so much for me. I was just entering the hormonal hell of puberty, not having a clue who I was, what I wanted to be, or even sometimes *what* I was. I was in the bloodsweats of anxiety, terrified by all the physical changes that were taking place in my body. I did not want them. "No" to the hairs that were appearing everywhere. "Yuck" to the globs of fat that appeared right onto the front of my chest.

In the fall of 1965, Aunt Mae and I began boarding with Uncle Jack's friend Ned and his wife, Flossy, on Cherry Hill Road after Aunt Mae sold the house on Rankin Street.* Their son, George,** who was in his early thirties, had come back from Ontario to live with his parents just before Christmas that year.

One day, around the middle of June 1966, I arrived home from school, and for no reason that was apparent to me, I was full of apprehension but still happy that summer was on its way. As I went to open the door, it swung toward me with great force. Flossy reached out and grabbed me violently by the arm and dragged me in over the doorstep, snarling, "You get in here." I tripped and stumbled into the front porch. Flossy was standing

---

* See Rankin Street info in "The Little Girl Who Grew Up Next Door to Her Family."
** Names have been changed to protect the guilty.

there in a red rage, glaring at me. Aunt Mae was standing behind Flossy, looking sadder than I'd ever seen her look. (Over the last year I had seen Aunt Mae look very, very sad indeed, so I knew something awfully bad was going on.) I looked at Aunt Mae and asked her, "What are you doing home from work so early? Are you okay?"

Aunt Mae nodded glumly and continued looking at me with even greater concern. Flossy, not able to control herself any longer, spat out, "You slut! What were you doing with George? I saw you. I followed George down to the school and I saw you get in the car, you little whore!"

I looked at her numbly, feeling nothing but horror. I instinctively stepped back and tripped over the threshold once again, barely keeping my feet. A wave of hot shame coursed through my entire body. I wanted to say something, but I was speechless. I would have run away, if only my feet would have moved. They wouldn't, and so I stood there, mute and paralyzed as Flossy called me every kind of bad word in the book. Finally, after what felt like an eternity, I went upstairs with Aunt Mae to our small, crowded bedroom, full to the ceiling of unpacked boxes of clothes, dishes, pots and pans, and God knows what else. My mind, in a frantic effort to get away from this horrible situation, busied itself with trying to figure out what was inside each box according to the note scrawled on the side. It wasn't a very effective form of escape, because, like a record stuck on repeat, I could still hear Flossy's words going over and over in my mind.

Aunt Mae limped over and put her arm around me. I didn't want her to, because that simple gesture immediately crumbled the wall I had been so furiously building. I wanted to protect myself against this shocking reality. A very small part of me felt like I was guilty—that I was all those words Flossy called me—but at the same time I knew I wasn't. I was being held responsible for something that was way beyond my level of understanding. I was only a little girl; I had just turned fourteen the month prior. I stood there, burning with the disgrace of being called those words even though a part of me knew I wasn't those words. At the same time, I thought: Why did I keep my rides with George a secret if they weren't bad, shameful, and disgraceful? My mind scrambled around in my head like one of those long pink-tailed rats on a wire wheel, unable to stop going around and around and around, and neither could my mind stop. I was searching for some escape from this awful situation.

Aunt Mae was saying something: "I called your mother and father. I told them everything. We agreed that the best thing for you is to go home to your mom and dad. A taximan will be here in a few minutes to take you Around the Bay to your mother's." I tried to rise up out of the coma of distress I was in, so I could protest this awful injustice. Even before I could get a word out, Aunt Mae was saying, "No, no, no, you've got to go home to your parents. I can't look after you anymore."

"But I don't want to go," I managed to stutter out.

Aunt Mae started to cry. "I don't know what to do. You're beyond me darling. You must see, don't you, that you can't stay here," she said, gesturing around the awful little room. "That's impossible now."

We stood saying nothing for what seemed like an eternity. I was hiccupping with sobs, and tears were running silently down Aunt Mae's cheeks. "I packed a little case for you," Aunt

Mae said, finally breaking the impasse and moving to the other side of the bed. I numbly reached out and took my little suitcase.

Before I could even say *But what about school?* or *What about all my things?* I found myself stuffed into the back seat of an around-the-bay taxi. Inside the 1963 Pontiac, there were twelve people packed in tighter than two coats of paint. Dick Nolan was singing that stupid Come Home Year song on a scratchy radio so loud I almost couldn't hear it, but I could still pick out those embarrassing lyrics: *Come Home to Newfoundland it's Come Home Year, all the Newfies will be gathered here. There's lots of fish and brewis and stuff like that, so don't stay where you're to, come where we're at.* The man driving the taxi was constantly picking his nose as if each nostril might be full of something so precious and worthwhile that he had to excavate it. Nobody but me seemed to mind or even take any notice. For a second my disgust distracted me from the situation at hand, but not for long. Soon I was thinking about how to kill myself in some non-scary, non-messy way, but unfortunately, every method of killing yourself seemed to be both scary and messy. I was squat in between two old women heading home from a day of shopping in town. I started to feel half sick. There was no air in the taxi and it felt like there was absolutely no air left in my life either.

When I arrived in on The Pinch, the unofficial name of the road where my family lived, got out of the taxi, and walked in the front door, full of fear and trepidation, almost immediately my family started making fun of me. On that very first day my mother said, referring to George and my three older sisters, "Well, he went after Madonna, then he chased after Lol and then Carol, and he finally got you." I knew she meant "got" in a way that was both dirty and shameful, and that's certainly how I felt, though I knew that in truth I'd never been "gotten." One of my brothers immediately started calling George "turkey neck"* and then all that summer whenever our paths crossed, which in that tiny, tiny little house happened constantly, he would break into a ditty he'd made up, singing, "Turk, turk, turk, turk-ey neeeeck" to the tune of "Turkey in the Straw." Every time it happened, I was mortified. On that first day it was made blatantly clear to me that, truly, I was worthless. I mean who gets given away** twice in one very short lifetime? It was obvious to me that only someone as deeply no good as fourteen-year-old me would ever have been sent to live with the very people who'd given her away in the first place. It's ironic that 1966 was Come Home Year, and people were coming home from everywhere, coming back to their natal seat to celebrate, to have fun, but I was coming home that year in sadness and disgrace.

Mom's house was tiny. Locally, we called houses like hers four-by-fours or Biscuit Box houses. There were four tiny bedrooms upstairs, a small front room, or parlour if you will, and a long, long kitchen that had once been two rooms. The wood stove took pride of place in the kitchen, which had a square Formica table and chair set, a day bed against one wall, and a homemade bench against the other. This was the room where everybody spent most of their time. There was no water or bathroom in Mom's house in 1966. Someone, usually my brother Frank, carried the water in big white salt beef buckets from the Mahoney's well next door. The Mahoneys had moved up to the

---

* In truth, George did have a neck that looked very much like a turkey's neck. He had almost no chin whatsoever. He was tall, lanky, old, and wildly unattractive.
** Or "thrown out" as my brother Greg recently put it.

Boston States years ago, but it was always a worrisome situation because Mom really didn't have any rights to that water. Big white salt beef buckets played a prominent role in Mom's house. There was one out in the back room that we used for slops, or if you really got caught out in the middle of the night and were afraid to go out in the pitch dark to the outhouse, you could use that. Oh, the outhouse! It was horrible. There were big black flies and it stunk. I had to hold my breath the whole time I was in there. Every part of my digestive system went on strike the first few weeks I was there, before they shut themselves down completely. Yes, everything about being sent home to Mom's was horrible, except for all the things about it that were wonderful.

I was a girl who had spent an inordinate amount of time upstairs alone on Carter's Hill in her big empty playroom, or sleeping in her equally large, empty bedroom, next to her old baby bedroom and the trunk room, all empty, all peopled just by me. Now I was in the midst of all this chaos, all this life, all this energy, all these people, coming and going at all hours of the day and night, and while it was totally overwhelming, it was exciting. When I arrived, there were already twenty or so people living, drinking, singing, fighting, sleeping, and eating in that massively small place. So many people in such a tiny house. It was immediately obvious that there was no room for me.

That first night there were so many people that Mom had to serve up supper in shifts. The first shift was for the Yanks who'd arrived home for Come Home Year, Mom's younger sister Aunt Cass, home from Brooklyn with her daughters, Mary and Laura, and Johnny, her youngest boy. In that first shift there was also Uncle Jack, who was in his fifties and still lived as a bachelor in a rooming house in Brooklyn. Uncle Jack, who would have to drink a full twenty-sixer of Canadian Club just to get ready to go out to the bar to have a few drinks. Uncle Jack, who drank a flask of whiskey every morning before he went up on the iron and always carried a flask in his toolbelt for courage. Uncle Jack, who was said to be one of the best connectors on any raising gang* in New York.

Also in the first shift: Ange Costello, a lovely warm woman from Camden who gave me the biggest smile when I arrived and said, "We're just home visiting from New Jersey for the summer, but, lucky you, you're home for good!" I imagine now that I tried to smile back but I know my heart sank when she said it. Her kindness made me feel even worse. Despite all the noise and the excitement, there was no getting away from the fact that my life as I knew it was over, and what lay ahead was looking long and bleak. Ange's two kids were with her, Mary, with whom I became great friends that summer, and Mary's drop-dead gorgeous brother, Davey. I immediately developed a major crush on Davey, despite my despair. He had the perfect look for the upcoming Summer of Love with his Donovan Leitch hat and his tumble of blonde curls. He looked like he could have been on the cover of *Tiger Beat*. He was a pubescent girl's dream fella.

I don't know who constituted the next shift, but I do remember that by the time I got to the table there was not much left. No roast, no chicken, just bones. I was outraged. I was used to being the cosseted only child in a house of adults. Adults who always wanted to make sure I had plenty to eat and was well taken care of. I burst into tears that night, more from anger and

---

* A raising gang is a specialized crew within the ironworkers' union that focusses on the initial stages of steel construction, including lifting and connecting steel pieces. They work at considerable heights.

hunger than anything else. Mom told me to fill up on bread and to stop bawlin', or she'd give me something to bawl about.

There were so many of us stuffed into that tiny house that summer. My oldest sister Madonna was home from Ontario. Madonna was sleeping in a tiny trailer in the backyard with her four youngsters but was eating and and mostly living with all and the rest of us in the house. My sister Laura was there, too, with her children Kim and Ronnie. There was Tom, my brophew, and Wanda, my sniece. Lol had Tom and Wanda when she was just a child herself, and so Mom and Dad had brought them up.* There was Aunt Cass and her three youngsters, and of course, Uncle Jack, my brothers Frank and Greg, Mom and Dad, and now me.

The first night I was there, Mom was having a big party for the Yanks** in the kitchen, where all parties were had.*** People were dancing, saying recitations (old pieces, like "The Boy Who Wore the Blue") and playing country music, which I hated.**** There was a fiddle and a guitar, played by Timmy Whalen and his son. That first night, I somewhat tentatively asked my mother where my room was. Mom, who never liked to be questioned

---

*   Later, if I thought about it at all, I could have felt resentful that they were brought up by Mom and Dad when I'd been given away, but Tom and Wanda were such a sweet and extraordinary pair, it was hard to work up any ill will toward them.

**   Dad always deeply resented the Yanks and their bragging about their derring-do on the high steel. With a few drinks in, he'd often remark, "I've been further aloft than any of ye Yankee bastards have been away from home."

*** "The heart of the Newfoundland household, centre for social activity. The parlour was available for more formal occasions but the kitchen was where families spent their time. Home of the stove and kettle—and the only warm room in the winter—it was where they ate and received visitors, where they had mug-ups between meals and napped on the daybed, where music and stories and other entertainment took place." Michael Crummey in *From This Place: Our Lives on Land and Sea*

**** In my own defense, I was very young, so didn't really get the whole country vibe, though I gotta say, I was pretty sad.

about anything, especially not at a party when she was having a good time, turned on me and said, "It's not your room, or my room, or his room—it's just whatever room you happen to end up in." I don't know how I happened to "end up" in the room I did, but by the time I got there it was already fully occupied: Tom, Wanda, and Kim were in the bed,* and Ronnie the baby was in a crib. I couldn't believe I had to get into an already full bed. Sharing the bed with Aunt Mae at Ned and Flossy's house had been awkward for me. I was so used to being alone that I feared any kind of close, physical contact, even with the people I loved. Sure, Carter's Hill had been lonely, but bonus: there was never anybody's smelly, big toe stuck up my nose. I didn't like this level of intimacy, or any level of intimacy, really, and I found the closeness both claustrophobic and mildly repulsive.

I had no sooner managed to get Tom's toe out of my nose, and keep it out, when Mom came in and got undressed. I didn't want to see my mother's bra and rubber girdle; it made me feel totally self-conscious and embarrassed. To me, it was like the horrible icing on the "too many people, too much chaos, too little in the way of space or privacy" cake. Then, she pushed me over out of the way and crawled into bed beside me. I had never been that physically close to my mother before, and now, here she was, in her bra and rubber girdle, spooned into the back of me. Just as I thought things couldn't get any worse in came my sister, Laura. She crawled into the head of the bed, next to Wanda, Kim, and Tom. I couldn't believe there were six of us in the bed. It's beyond comprehension where all those

---

* Wanda always burned hot, so she was great to share a bed with in the winter, but in the summer, oh boy! Boiling.

people managed to fit in that tiny house. It was like a jigsaw puzzle, but one with too many pieces and too few beds or rooms to fit them in.

Even if we were all sleeping on the floor, it would have been tight. That night, Aunt Cass, Laura, and Mary must've been in one room; Johnny was in with Greg and Frank; and Dad was always alone in his room with his bottles of Captain Morgan, which were actually bottles of pee because sometimes he'd refuse to come downstairs, even to use the slops bucket in the back room. Madonna and her four youngsters were out in the trailer, and all the rest of us were in the room where I was. For the second time in one long, long day, I found myself squat into a place where there really was no room for me.

That night, trying to go to sleep, I burned with shame as I remembered the events that had brought me back to my parents' house. I remembered how awful things were living with Flossy and Ned who didn't like me at all, and how I was desperate not to be there. I was an adolescent girl who spent every free moment on the phone. It was my lifeline. Sometimes I'd stay on the phone saying nothing, just knowing I was connected to one of my friends, freed from the awful prison of that house. Just feeling that connection, the chance to be linked to someone who understood all the big thoughts and feelings and wants that were rattling around inside of my inflamed pubescent brain. All those big feelings and emotions had no means of escape except for me to stay on the phone, hour after hour, talking to one of my friends about how gorgeous the Hawley twins were or how, really, John was so much cuter than Paul, and did you see how greasy Debbie's hair was today, you could fry an egg in all that grease . . . Somehow, that would comfort me and turn down all that rattling noise and fear and the terrible not knowing of being a thirteen-year-old girl.

In those days, there was only one phone per house, and my long and constant calls were a big and continuing source of friction on Cherry Hill Road. One time, at Flossy and Ned's, I answered the phone, and a Mrs. Hunt asked me to let Flossy know that she'd called. I was distracted, thinking about the glorious Hawley twins, Keith and Karl, who all the grade eight girls at Mercy Convent were madly in love with. Sadly, it looked like Bonnie White had Keith and Karl was my friend Maureen's boyfriend. And so, it was just unrequited love on my part, the saddest and most distracting kind of love. That year there was a tall, lanky, gawky-looking guy. He was a bit twerpy, but I was 5'8" and at least he was taller than me, and I knew, even at that time—maybe more then than ever—that, as the Ron Hynes song says, there was no point in my "dreaming beyond my expectations." I'd written his name all over my binder in pink nail polish, hoping he'd notice, and also to let everyone know that, even though I didn't have a boyfriend, I was determined to get one by hook or by crook. I was thirteen for heaven's sake, and everybody else had boyfriends. Anyway, this is what I was thinking about when I told the lady on the phone, "All right, Mrs. Cunt, I'll tell her."

It wasn't until Mrs. Hunt gasped that I realized what I'd said. Well, the whole house went mad about that. It was impossible to explain to Flossy or Ned or even Aunt Mae that it had been just a slip of the tongue, and that I would never in all of my life say *that* word, that *awful, awful* word. "Well, you can see what kind of a filthy cesspool her mind is," Flossy said. Her opinion of me was already very low, but after that call, it went underground. "She only got one thing on that brain!" Aunt Mae was taken aback, and she was disappointed and embarrassed, but not half as embarrassed as I was. I didn't even know where the word had come from and I didn't say it again for another thirty years or so.*

Flossy was a thin, severe, bespectacled middle-aged woman and Ned, who inexplicably went around the house without his shirt on most of the time, his big hard beer belly and his hairy chest out for all the world to see, looked more like a longshoreman than you could ever imagine a longshoreman would look. Mostly I hated it there, and Flossy and Ned weren't exactly thrilled to have Aunt Mae and I as boarders either. Then their son George came home from Toronto. George was tall and thin, with a big nose and seemingly no chin whatsoever. Flossy treated him as if he was the most precious thing that had ever existed in her world, and she lit up like a Christmas tree whenever she clapped eyes on him. She was beside herself with joy to have him home. On first viewing, I didn't really see anything worth getting lit up about. On that first night he was home, he caught my eye and held it for a little too long. I felt uncomfortable and I wasn't sure where to look. I admit, I did also feel a tiny thrill that I was getting attention from a fella, even an old fella with what my family always later referred to as "a turkey neck."

George took an active interest in me. He wanted to know what I was reading. He offered to help me with my math homework, but he was no good at math either and that made me see him as a "human" and not so much as a "grown up." He would sit with me at the kitchen table when I was doing my homework

---

* Now I prefer the word "cunt" to "bitch" because, you know, I'm not a female dog and never will be, but I do at least have a cunt, and it's—as Cathy Jones always says—a beautiful thing.

and often Flossy would be at the stove scowling in my direction, remarking that George must have had better things to be at than grade eight arithmetic.

Then one day at recess when all us grade eighters were out in the playground, our koolituks* and winter coats covering up our schoolgirl, navy serge uniforms, with the white buttons down the front and the plastic collars and cuffs, I was playing a very intense game of Russians and Americans. Libby Ring was a Russian and I played the heroic American who had captured the bad Russian, who I was now dragging around the snow-covered playground by her hood.** Libby had started yelling out "Stop! Stop!" in a kind of strangled voice but I didn't pay any attention. I was intent on bringing my prisoner back to the American base. As we went past Sister Mary Corona, who was not fully a nun yet and so put on playground duty, she stopped me. "Look! Look what you're doing!"

She slapped my hand to make me let go of Libby's hood, but I still held on, deep in the game and determined to win. After Sister Corona took me by the shoulders and shook me quite violently, though, I had to let Libby go. Libby was coughing and clawing at her neck, trying to loosen the chord tied under her chin to keep the hood on. Sister Corona's face was red with anger, and she was right up in my face, screaming, covering me in nun spit. As I drew back, a horn beeped, and I looked up and saw it was George, driving his old Chev. Thinking something must be wrong with Aunt Mae, I turned on my heel and ran away from Sister Corona and toward the car.

---

* A style of parka, very popular in the mid-'60s.
** I often get carried away, and way too committed to the game or the work or whatever.

When I got there, George smiled up at me. I could hear Sister Corona calling out my name, but I ignored it. I asked George if anything was wrong with Aunt Mae. He said, "No, no, nothing's wrong, I just thought I'd drop by and see how things were going. Did ya get back your mark on that arithmetic test?"

"No, not yet," I answered, taken aback that some adult, not Aunt Mae, would remember that I had an arithmetic test.

"Get in for a minute," George said, "we'll take a spin around the block."

"Oh, I'm not sure, recess is almost over. The little kids are lining up to go back in."

"Come on," George said. "We won't be long." As I got in the car, he asked me, "What are you reading now?"

"*Tomorrow Will Be Sunday*,* you know, that—"

"Oh, the dirty book," George interrupted, giving me a look I couldn't quite interpret. "Isn't that a bit too grown up for a little girl like you?"

"No," I said as I got in the car. "I'm allowed to read whatever I like. They moved me up into the big library. I probably already read everything downstairs in the kid's library." I was so proud of that. I had been anxiously awaiting the opportunity to let someone know that even though I was only in grade eight I was already a member of the adult library. "I'm going to take out *Catcher in the Rye* next."

"Well, all the dirty books," he said, giving me that odd look again.

I felt very nervous as we drove around the block, and when

---

* *Tomorrow Will Be Sunday*, by Newfoundland author Harold Horwood, caused significant controversy upon its release due to its explicit, lewd themes that included sexual content.

we got back to the front gate, there was no one left on the playground. I panicked. I reached to open the door and George quickly leaned over and kissed me, just a quick kiss but right on the lips. It was shocking. It brought me to a full stop. I had so many feelings rushing through me that I got weak. I tried to open the door and fell back against the seat.

George said, "You liked that did you?" I didn't know whether I did like it or not. I managed to gather the bits of myself together as best I could and I opened the door, flew out of the car and into the school. I was in a daze at school the rest of that morning. I was so confused by what had happened with George. I didn't like it. It's true that I did want someone to kiss me, but not George, and it was so weird for him to show up at recess.

After that first visit, almost every day for the rest of that year George came to pick me up either at recess or after school. On a couple of days, one or two of the girls from class would come with us. But when I was alone with George, well, the kissing kept going. There was no intimate touching or anything beyond necking, but I began to feel increasingly uncomfortable. And back at the house, with Flossy and Ned and Aunt Mae, George would often wink at me when he thought they weren't looking. I knew he was implying something, but I was never quite sure what that something was. It made me blush up to the roots of my hair and feel terribly queasy and butterfly-y in my stomach. I wrote in my diary all about George and the drives in his car, but nothing about how worried and uneasy I was becoming. I hid my diary as best I could, upstairs under the mattress in the little room Aunt Mae and I shared.

And so the spring that I turned fourteen played itself out full of fun trips to Bowring Park, and with drives down unexplored dirt roads or out to the A&W drive-in. I began to get the sense that George was pushing me in some way and that maybe I owed him for all the adventures and all the drives, and the uncommon interest he showed in me and in my math homework. I was beginning to think that maybe I should be more forthcoming with my modest and awkward kisses. But I didn't want to, after all, even French-kissing was a mortal sin, and so guaranteed you an eternity of suffering the unspeakable tortures of the damned, and I did not want that.

Once during that spring, four of my classmates all jammed into the back of George's car. Everyone was in high spirits: the sludge, ice, and snow of the St. John's spring was melting and running in the streets, and the temperature was unseasonably warm. I was wearing my brand-new, vinyl yellow coat that I'd somehow managed to convince Aunt Mae to buy for me. I had seen such vinyl coats in *Seventeen* magazine. Pierre Cardin had come out with the first one and Aunt Mae had bought me one of the only two high fashion vinyl coats that Bowring Brothers had in stock.

I was so happy that morning. We all went to Bowring Park and we climbed the Peter Pan statue down by the Swan's Pond.

We were on the pip* for the rest of that day, and at the end of it, we went back into school just to get our books and stuff. When we arrived in the cloakroom, we found the rest of the grade eighters in a tizzy. Everyone had seen my new vinyl coat that morning and they'd loved it so much they'd talked about it all day. Sister Pauline had overheard them and realized that I was missing. She then discovered that Susan, Maureen, Janet, and the other girl were also missing. At that point, Sister Pauline

---

* On the pip: skipping school.

walked into the cloakroom and demanded to see us right away over at the convent. My heart plummeted right into my sensible black lace-up brogues, and together we all headed over.

Not one of us wanted to knock on that imposing black door. None of us had ever actually called at the convent before. Finally, I stepped up and knocked on the door. Immediately, as if she'd been waiting on the other side, Sister Pauline came out. She was angry but said that she was more disappointed than anything else. She'd been worried about us all day and had been about to call our parents. She said she was placing us in detention for the rest of the year. I felt a bit like we were getting away with it, because, really, there was hardly any "rest of the year" left. Then Sister Pauline said none of us would be allowed to take part in the grade eight graduation, our last official event at Mercy Convent. We were all very, very disappointed because we'd already got our white dresses and matching shoes to wear to the commencement ceremony. Still, I thought it could have been much worse. As I was heading out through the gate, however, the arm of my brand new beautiful and perfect yellow vinyl coat got caught on the sharp iron spikes of the gate and tore apart. At the time I thought, well, even if that was the worst that came out of it, then I'd still really managed to get away lightly. Looking back, though, I can see now that it was the beginning of the inevitable end.

One day, as recess began, I was waiting for George at the gates of the Mercy Convent playground. That day I felt sort of unsettled. I could tell that something was wrong, but I didn't know what.* I also knew I didn't really have the courage to look

---

* I sometimes wonder if I suffer from a little of the second sight that my grandfather possessed.

at whatever it might be. So still wearing my beautiful vinyl yellow coat, which Aunt Mae had done her best to mend and restore to its former glory, I hopped in the front seat. I didn't want to go for a drive that day, and I said to George that I didn't want to go anywhere and asked George if we could just stay there in front of the school for recess.

I turned on the radio and heard the Monkees song "Last Train to Clarksville." It was number one that spring on the local radio station VOCM's Top Ten. I was glued to VOCM's Top Ten when I wasn't glued to the phone, and I knew the words to all the songs. I couldn't help but sing along, "You can be here by four-thirty 'cause I've made your reservation." In response to my singing, George always said something dismissive, almost contemptuous, of the Monkees and the Dave Clarke Five, or whatever band I'd loved at the time. George would laugh at me and tell me that I didn't like real music, only Bopper music. He said that day that the Monkees weren't even a real band, only a bunch of *talente-libre* nobodies who were brought together to make a TV show. I didn't know what *talente-libre* meant, but I was mildly impressed by it because it sounded foreign and sophisticated. George was always proving how much smarter he was than me, and how much more he knew. But that day, I felt particularly vulnerable, and I burst into tears when George said that about the Monkees. That didn't stop him from making fun of me and my love for "garbage Bopper music." It did occur to me then that I was a Bopper, and so what kind of music was I supposed to love?

I was at that age when everyone is so uncomfortable, and so not settled in their own skin, because I was so tall, and because I was brought up by three adults, and appeared to be so mature/

precocious, people were always telling me, in no uncertain terms: "A big girl like you, grow up for God's sakes and stop actin' like a little youngster." Everyone wanted me to be older than I was, more mature than I was, a different person than I was, and I did try. I really did.

Finally, that day, recess was over. I didn't think anything of it at the time but as I was getting out of the car, I caught sight of a thin, bespectacled woman disappearing down the alley across the street from the school. I only got a brief glimpse of the retreating figure but something about the woman reminded me of Flossy. I didn't think any more about it just then, though, and went back into the school.

All that long afternoon after George left, I continued to feel unsettled. I didn't want to be home, and I didn't want to be in school either. It seemed that afternoon that I didn't want to be anywhere. I would have liked to have disappeared if that was an option, but that wasn't possible.

THOUGH I SWORE THE FIRST NIGHT THAT I STAYED with Mom and them that I would never be able to sleep, I was soon off in dreamland. That summer, my mother's house was alive with people: sometimes violent people, but always funny people, sarcastic people, drunk people, people who were ready to mock you as soon as look at you. Coming from the deep quiet of my previous life, and also the shame of recent events, a part of me welcomed the chaos, even though sometimes it was terrifying. I missed my life with Aunt Mae, and I missed Aunt Mae herself, particularly when things were bad. Like the one night my two hugely pregnant sisters got into a fistfight and ended up rolling around on the floor. Their baby bumps kept them slightly more apart than they were determined to be as they screamed insults and cursed at each other, trying to tear each other's hair out. That was a sight that imprinted itself on my retina and disturbed me so deeply that I couldn't stop crying and repeating that I wanted to go home. No one listened at all; everyone was too intent on breaking up the racket between Madonna and Lol.

I don't remember all the details about that summer, just the extremes of emotion and a few events that stood out in stark relief. One night, I went over to a woman's house in Avondale, the next community south of Conception Harbour. I don't remember now how I got there. She was a woman my brother, Mike, was involved with at the time. While I was there, I drank whiskey for the first time in my life. I got so drunk and so happy that I got down on the floor, crawling around in glee, completely out of it. Someone gave me a ride home, back to The Pinch, and I think I was kissing the driver when both my older sisters came down and with great drama violently opened both front doors of the car. Lol reached in and hauled me out, and Madonna yelled something at the driver before she slammed the door with great force.

My sisters marched me upstairs into the room where Mom was in bed. Because of the whiskey, all I remember is that Mom slapped me hard across the face. That totally knocked me for a loop. No one had ever slapped me across the face before; there was very little, if any, slapping that went on in my previous life. When I came downstairs from the slapping, my sister, Lol, called me a bad name—the same one that Flossy had flung at me that awful day. I said, "Well, at least I didn't get knocked up when I was fifteen!" Lol flew across the kitchen at me, wielding an iron frying pan. Luckily, Dad had come downstairs and stepped in between us. I was drunk and sobbing wildly and Dad put his arm around me and said I should sleep out in Madonna's trailer that night. As he was walking me back there, trying to stop me from sobbing, I think he said that he loved me. Subconsciously, the connection between drinking whiskey and getting love remained strong in me for years.

Aunt Cass's son, Johnny, was about ten years old at this time and cute as a button. He was also a tantalizer and a crucifier, and he spent that summer calling us "Goofie Newfies." I remember one day Greg was wearing a shirt that had come from the States in a bag. (The American aunts and cousins were always sending home used but sometimes quite beautiful things to poor us, still stuck here on the rock.) One day when Johnny was yelling "Goofie Newfies" at us, I pushed him and said, "Stop saying Goofie Newfies!" and he said in his strong Brooklyn accent, "Why? That's what you are! You got nothin' but outhouses, you're just stupid! Have you ever been on a roller coaster on Coney Island? Ever been on the subway? Ever even been in a city?" And I said, "Yeah! I live in a city! And my dad says that St. John's was a city when New York was a mud hole." And Johnny of course, quick as a wink, said, "Yeah. And now New York is a city and St. John's is a mud hole. You live in a shithole and shit in an outhouse, Gewwww-fie Newwww-fies." He pointed at the shirt my brother Greg was wearing and said, "That shirt was mine, but I never wanted to wear it. Only a

Goofie Newfie'd wear a shirt like that." After that, Greg took a flying leap at Johnny and knocked him to the ground. Greg ripped off the shirt he was wearing, tore it to shreds, and tried to stuff it down Johnny's mouth. I, fully in support of this effort, was holding Johnny down, both of us going at it with a vengeance.

Aunt Cass stormed out of the house and pulled me and Greg off Johnny. She turned on me then, saying, "Oh my! You're gone mad all together! Poor little fella. Never done you no harm. Big old thing like you picking on a little fella like him." Johnny was still on the ground, still chanting "Goofie Newfie!" Did I mention that Aunt Cass was deaf? She was deadly at reading lips, could even read them from a hundred yards away, but I guess she chose not to read Johnny's that day.*

Mary Ryan, Aunt Cass's daughter, was two years older than me. I was so jealous of her and I resented her on sight. She knew all the new dances: the boogaloo, the wahtoosie, the mashed potato, and all the others, most of which we'd never even heard of in Newfoundland yet. She arrived in a white eyelet crop top and white bell-bottom pants, neither of which was available, to the best of my knowledge, in any store anywhere on the island. I'd seen something like them in *Seventeen*, but to see them, right there in Mom's kitchen on an actual human being, my gob was smacked. Worse than all that though was the fact that Mom seemed to like her a lot. She

---

* The last song Aunt Cass heard before she went deaf was "Constantinople" by Paul Whiteman, which she would belt out every time she had a few drinks in. "C-O-N-S-T-A-N-T-I-N-O-P-L-E! Constantinople!" she'd roar. Always loud, always off-key. Then Mom would roll her eyes and say, "Somebody hit me in the back of the head with a fuckin' chair!"

liked the sauciness of her, the always ready with a quick quipness of her. All summer long, every fella I developed a crush on (which would include any fella between Harbour Main and Brigus, under the age of eighteen, with a pulse) she ended up going out with.

Once at one of Mom's parties, I slept out in Madonna's trailer. The party was going full force when an old fella with a bald head and a very off-putting giggle came into the trailer and tried to crawl into bed and get on top of me. I was horrified. I don't know if I screamed or what happened, but Mom came in laughing and grabbed him by the scruff of the neck, saying, "T . . . you old goat, get off her!" Then she laughed some more and gave me a hard look for screaming.

At the end of the summer there was the annual Parish Garden Party. What an event! It caused such excitement in the house on The Pinch. The Garden Party was always the first Sunday in August. After mass and a huge Sunday dinner, usually consisting of at least one chicken and a small roast (pork or beef), and a big aluminum boiler-full of cabbage, turnip, carrot, salt meat, peas pudding, and maybe even a blueberry duff, all boiled up together in a massive pot, everyone would head back down to the church grounds for the Garden Party. Just as everyone was leaving, Mom said I had to stay home and wash the dishes first. By that time, I was so used to being treated unfairly,* I barely argued—just enough so that my older brother Mike gave me a big smack across the face. Smacks across the

---

* I always felt, for years, that my having to do the dishes was some sort of unnatural punishment forced on me by an unjust God. I think this incident may have been the genesis of those feelings.

face were quite common in on The Pinch. When I finally got to the Garden Party, though, it was magical.

The sun was shining, people were dressed in their best, tickets on kewpie dolls and all manner of wonderful things were being sold hand over fist. But the pièce de résistance was something they called the Swinging Boat. The Swinging Boat was a large wooden structure that swung back and forth, manned on both sides by men of the parish who would pull on the rope to make the boat swing higher and higher. Depending on how drunk the men might be, it could become a very dangerous ride. That August in 1966 my sisters Madonna and Lol went off somewhere, leaving me in charge of all the youngsters. I got them on board the Swinging Boat, and we were having the time of our lives when I spotted Davey Costello, or was it my cousin Ed? Or Paul O'Driscoll, or any one of the numberless fellas I had a crush on that summer. Anyway, I stopped paying any attention to the youngsters. I didn't want to be babysitting in the first place, but people kept leaving them in my charge. It's not like I ever put much effort into looking after those youngsters, on the supposition, I guess, that if I did the job badly enough I wouldn't be asked to do it again. That didn't usually hold true in Mom's house. There, if you did a job badly enough, you had to do it again, and you had to take on even bigger jobs as punishment for having done a bad job on the first one.

But that day, as I was gazing lovingly at the object of my adolescent affections, the Swinging Boat rope wrapped itself around my brophew Tom's little neck. No one noticed that he was choking and on the verge of being hung. Thank God I finally did. I got to him, stopped the Swinging Boat, and somehow freed him from the rope. He still has a scar on his neck from that Sunday.*

The whole summer was like that: full of fun and tragic events. I found it so hard to get my feet. I never felt up to the task at hand. I just couldn't find my way in, and I never felt like I was part of my family. I desperately wanted to be part of them, but at the same time, I profoundly didn't want to be part of them, and I wanted to go home, back to Aunt Mae.

That summer was one of the worst summers of my entire life and also one of the most exciting. I suddenly had so much freedom, and there were so many people, so much noise, so much life. Mom used to make my older brother Frank take me to dances with him and all his friends. Because it was Come Home Year, there were dances almost every night. Wednesday night, street dance in Brigus. Thursday night, a dance in Manuals. Friday night, on the wharf in Holyrood. That summer, I became close friends with Mary Costello from Camden and Mary Dalton, my sweet natured lovely cousin who lived next door. Together, we took ownership of the mountain that rose up behind Mom's house and we called it the 3M Mountain, and we were the 3M Club. And there was swimming and the Overfalls and wiener roasts and bonfires, and walking to Avondale in the pitch

---

* Mom was with the other parish ladies serving up turkey teas (sometimes called a Cold Plate here on the island). She'd made her famous potato salad and was dressed in quite a fancy blue dress with a matching voile apron. She did look quite fetching and that made me even angrier with her. Everyone was mad at me, which seemed so deeply unfair and unjust. I remember thinking at the time, "Why is it my job to look after them? They're not my youngsters." I simply did not understand the situation my poor sisters found themselves in. I had no sympathy whatsoever. I had no room for it. All my sympathy, all my pity, was wrapped up in myself (typical adolescent I guess). But sadly, I managed to stay in that awful, adolescent state until I was forty and stopped drinking.

dark, and fellas, always new fellas from Pittsburgh and Brooklyn and Brigus and going to those dances, and no one ever asking you to dance.

By the end of August, Aunt Mae had found a small apartment on Henry Street and somehow or other, I managed to convince her to let me come home. So just before school started, in that same taxi, I headed back home, but the notion of home, which is generally defined as some place that always has to let you in, was forever destroyed for me that summer, and I realized that I didn't really have a home or belong anywhere. I had started drinking and smoking, and I'd gotten seduced by all the noise and all the rackets and all the bright aliveness of my family's dysfunction, and even though I wanted to go back to Aunt Mae, some part of me was desperate to leave the quiet sadness of my former life behind. I didn't want to stay with them, but I wanted to be them.

Makin' Time with the Yanks

DAD ALWAYS SAID, "IF YOU CAN'T GET A MAN, GET A Yank," and at one point, here in Newfoundland, there were plenty of Yanks to get. Early in the Second World War, before the United States joined the war effort, Great Britain gave the U.S., rent-free, ninety-nine-year leases on land in Newfoundland and Labrador on which they could build military bases. In exchange, the U.S. gave Britain much-needed warships and destroyers. The Americans built the Pepperell Air Force Base in St. John's, an army airfield in Goose Bay, another in Stephenville, and a naval station in Argentia, making us one of the most highly militarized places in North America. So, according to what you can hear, by 1941 Newfoundland was crawling with Yanks, Nylons, Chocolates, and "Whiskey for your father." A woman who spent the war years in St. John's described those years to me as "dancing, dancing, dancing, five years of non-stop dancing."

Oh, the Yanks, no one could get over the look of them, the length and the breadth of them. "Look at the teeth on 'em" was as far as I could tell the most oft repeated comment made about them by Newfoundlanders.

At that time, Winston Churchill personally thanked Newfoundlanders for the land he gave away to the Americans without our consent. "For the sake of the Empire, of Liberty, and of the welfare of all mankind, thank you," he said.

The first Americans arrived on the luxury ship the *Edmund B. Alexander* out of New York. They pulled into St. John's during Lent in 1941.* There were at one point more than 100,000 American military troops stationed in Newfoundland. It was a Yankapalooza. During the war years, it seemed that every young Newfoundland woman had at least seven American boyfriends, plus their Newfoundland fiancé, who were fighting over in France or cutting wood in Scotland. In Newfoundland, we referred to the arrival of the Yanks as "the friendly invasion."

The arrival of the Americans brought Newfoundland a much-needed economic boom. We were dead broke and could not manage our debt payments. Back in the early '30s, Britain had agreed to help Newfoundland with its debt, with the proviso that they would have complete political control over the colony to protect their investment. After seventy-nine years of responsible government, in 1933 the democratically elected Newfoundland Legislature voted itself out of existence.

The Dominion of Newfoundland was no more. No elec-

---

* "Holy Mother Church says don't dance during Lent. That's the kind of rules that's meant to be bent. The Yanks got the moola, that's gotta be spent. Stateside is gone, but this burgh is bent."—Opening song from the collective play *Makin' Time with the Yanks*.

tions took place, and no legislature was convened, for the next fifteen years. We became an island run by seven commissioners appointed by the British government. We were reduced, once again, to a Crown colony. This second colonization was designed to give us, according to the Brits, "a much-needed rest from politics."

Growing up, I felt mortified that we Newfoundlanders, without a fight, without even a whimper, had given up on the notion of governing ourselves and had seen ourselves as incapable of taking part in a democratic system. A country that voluntarily gives up self-government is unusual, but many societies gave up faith in democratic institutions during the Great Depression.*

But I knew nothing of this back in 1959, when I was in grade one at Our Lady of Mercy Convent and I was delighted to have two American girls in my class, Anne Marie Dorothy and Helen Hayes (I had no idea that there was a famous actress by this name). I was totally taken with them, as were we all. Firstly, because they were American, they didn't have to kneel when saying the morning, noon, and afternoon prayers; and, secondly, because of who they were they got away with everything. At one point, Helen Hayes, who was all we thought an American would be—brash, brave, and loud—crept up behind Sister Maria Concepta, our grade one teacher, and pulled off her long black veil. We were all kneeling with our eyes closed, saying our morning prayers. Sister Maria Concepta's gasp made us all look up: there was Sister Concepta with her white wimple exposed. We were in shock. We couldn't imagine what bad

---

* See Germany and Italy.

things were going to happen to poor little Helen Hayes, but because she was one of the Yanks, and because she was from the base, she didn't even receive the mildest rebuke. Proof positive that it was great to be an American.

At the end of the school day, a big grey American Forces bus picked up all their kids from the St. John's schools and brought them back to the base. Once, Anne Marie Dorothy—who was the opposite of Helen Hayes, very quiet, very mousy—asked me if I wanted to go have a sleepover at her apartment on the base. I was beyond thrilled.* That Friday afternoon, I got on that big grey bus with all the American kids and rode all the way down to Fort Pepperell. That night, we ate at the PX (the post exchange, or the commissary on American bases). I think I had something called a Western sandwich, which was brand new to me and so very exciting. Then we went back to Anne Marie's family's apartment. I don't think I'd ever been in an apartment before, let alone one that was chock-a-block with whole cartons of gum and flats of Coca-Cola. I was agog. Then the phone rang. It was Aunt Mae. I'd forgotten to tell anyone that I was going to Anne Marie's for the weekend and they were beside themselves. Anne Marie's parents were somewhat taken aback and a little angry. I'm not sure how I got home—maybe Anne Marie's father had a car, or maybe they put me in a taxi—but I do know that they never invited me back again. That was the first experience I had Makin' Time with the Yanks.

By the time I'd grown into a young woman and was actively out looking for a fella—any fella'd do—Fort Pepperell

---

* Although I remember wishing it had been Helen who invited me. I never wanted what I had, I always wanted what I didn't have.

had closed. Goose Bay, Gander, and Stephenville had all been demobilized and the only base left was the naval base in Argentia. One Christmas, in those dead days between Christmas Day and New Year's, me and the Three Musketeers—that's what my friends Ester, Trallee, and Pat called themselves—went hitchhiking. (Counting me there were four musketeers, but I guess they weren't counting me.)* Oh, the muck and the misery of Christmas! Christmas, Our Lord's revenge for the crucifixion. I felt the saddest at Christmas because I imagined everyone else's Christmas to be one glorious Christmassy event after another—riding in one-horse open sleighs, laughing all the way, surrounded by family and loved ones.** By the time I was hitchhiking on Topsail Road with the girls, I was sixteen, and the Christmas pall became thicker and darker and sadder the older I got.

We were hitchhiking home from Mount Pearl in front of the Pink Poodle restaurant when a car of American sailors stopped and picked us up. They were driving a small black Volkswagon Beetle and how we all fit in there was beyond me. The sailors were on their way in from Argentia to spend their 80s*** in St. John's. There were four of us and four of them. Normally we wouldn't get in a car with that many guys, but they all looked so cute. I still dimly remember them in those adorable American sailor suits. There was a Hawaiian guy. Hardy was his name. Him I remember so well. He was huge—not fat, just big. I don't

---

* The fourth musketeer in the story was D'Artagnan, whom some people believe was the most important musketeer. Of course I never mentioned this to Pat, Trollee, or Ester. I kinda knew how they'd take it.
** At that time I was practically drowning in self-pity.
*** A term commonly used in the 1960s by the sailors in Argentia to describe their time off.

remember the other two, but there was one for each of us. I ended up with the driver, a guy named Tom. He was from Chicago and wore glasses and was short.

He seemed sweet, though, and he also seemed to be taken with me. These two things put me off him right away. Like Groucho Marx, I didn't want to be part of any club that would have me for a member. But like I already said, under the circumstances,* any fella would do, and so Tom it was. He was a big reader, too, so we had lots to talk about. I think he would have been a hippie if he hadn't been in the Navy. After that initial meeting, I started going out with him whenever he was in town for his 80s—well, kind of.

I didn't really go out with him, because I was ashamed of him. He was too short, wore dorky glasses, and liked reading. He was too much like the me I desperately didn't want to be. But the biggest problem with Tom was that he liked me. So what kind of a pathetic loser must he be? But we'd go to movies and hang out at Aunt Mae's and my apartment on Henry Street. I remember seeing *Bonnie and Clyde* with him. He saw the film as a metaphor for American society, whereas all I saw was how exquisite Faye Dunaway looked in all those berets and hats, and how much I longed to look like that.

Sometimes (but not very often) I would deign to be seen out in a bar with Tom, joining the three musketeers and their fellas, and some weekends us girls would hitchhike down to the base, rent one room for the four of us at a motel in Placentia, and stay out there for the weekend. I'm not sure what I told Aunt Mae

---

* The circumstances being I seemed to be the only girl in the entire world without a boyfriend.

about what I was doing or where I was going. I wasn't sleeping with Tom, although I'd already disastrously lost my virginity in the back of my friend Shelia's boyfriend's father's car.*

On May 13, 1969, I was turning seventeen. Like that Joni Mitchell song "Down to You," for me everything came and went marked by lovers but mostly styles of clothes. I remember vividly what I was wearing on that birthday: it was a micro-mini, yellow, long-sleeved dress with a white-lace bib front; very, very short, and so it was a bad dress to get loaded in. It had very little coverage. Because it was my birthday, I got really, really drunk—although even at seventeen, it didn't have to be my birthday for me to get really, really drunk. I had gotten Tom to set up a date for my best friend, Maureen, so he brought his friend Bob Brownlee along.

We went to the A&W in Bob's car. It, too, was a VW Beetle, but a much newer one than Tom's. It's hard today to impress on anyone what a big deal the A&W was to us at that time. It was the very first drive-in on the island, and the servers wore roller skates and hung your food on a tray from your car window. I ordered the Chubby Chicken, and I kept choking because I was so drunk and the chicken was so dry. Bob Brownlee was tall, and he paid absolutely no attention to me whatsoever, no matter how much I choked or writhed around drunkenly on the back seat. He seemed cold and self-contained. I was immediately in love.

Bob and Tom were on different work schedules, so their time off came at different times of the week. I began to date them both.

I went on like this until one disastrous weekend when Tom

---

* See "Write What You Know."

invited me to a special party at the base. He came into town and picked me up, and when we arrived at the base, much to my consternation, Bob was there. I never expected to see him, and I didn't know what to do or where to turn. It was an existential crisis of the highest order. I didn't have a clue who I really wanted to be with.* I immediately started to drink heavily and concocted a mad plan to walk out into the ocean the same way Virginia Woolf had walked out into that river. I wouldn't put any rocks in my pockets though, because I was planning on being saved. I thought whoever saved me, Tom or Bob, was who I'd decide to be in love with. In 1969, wide-legged bell-bottoms were extraordinarily popular, and this was the style of work dungarees American sailors wore. Tom had given me two or three pairs, one of which I was wearing that day. I remember thinking somewhat groggily as I walked out into the ocean that they couldn't have been good pants for sailors. As they got wetter and wetter, the deeper they kept dragging me into the ocean. But bravely—or actually, ridiculously—I kept on going.

Of course, it was Tom who swam out to save me and hauled me back to shore. I didn't want him to save me, but I'm not sure whether Bob, in his cold aloofness, even noticed that I was drowning. Being nothing if not stubborn and persistent, I decided to go out again. This time I let Bob know I was going into the water and I was going to do away with myself. Once again, Tom saved me. I didn't bother going in for a third dip—even in my drunken stupor I knew it would be Tom who saved me. But my mind was made up. Bob was the person I was in love with and with whom I wanted to be.

---

* I'd never heard of polyamory at that point.

Soon after, I ended up sleeping with Bob. The first time we had sex he left his black socks on, which is really all I remember about it, except that it happened at the Welcome Hotel, which was as seedy a downtown hotel as we had in St. John's at that time. Bob gave me his high school ring. I don't have much memory of what he and I did together. I know he raced his little blue Beetle in some off-road events that I attended, and he and some other guys had an apartment up behind the Avalon Mall. I hung out there a bit, and I remember hearing Led Zeppelin for the first time in that apartment and hating the band. By the end of that summer, Bob's time was getting short, which meant his time in Argentia was coming to an end and he was being reassigned to a base in Hawaii.

But first he was given a month off, so he was going back to Denver to spend time with his family. I don't know how it happened, but I was going to Denver with him. Even though I sometimes behaved like a lunatic, a lot of the time I wanted to live just like a conservative 1950s housewife. Because I had slept with Bob, I felt that we had to get married. I'm not sure what Bob felt, or if I even cared. Late in the summer, Bob and I got on a plane and headed off to meet his family. I'd never been anywhere farther from St. John's than Conception Harbour.* Before I left, I had a special travelling outfit made: a royal blue gilet, with white, wide-legged cuffed pants, made of the same fabric as the gilet. I felt I was well-enough dressed to take on the wide world, or at least Denver.

So this was my first major trip away from home, and it was

---

* Oh no, that's not true. Me and the girls sometimes used to hitchhike to Gander, get a plate of chips, gravy, and dressing, and then hitchhike home again.

to America. America, the place that occupied such a huge space in my head.* Everything good came out of America: music, all the groovy dances, hippies, all the Hollywood stars, all the great movies, all the innovations. The Vietnam War did cast a somewhat dark pall over American fabulousness. I had protested the war earlier that year at the American embassy in St. John's. With the crowd, I helped turn over a car; it was the first time I was ever part of a mob. I remember feeling such excitement, I remember the thrill and the wonder of feeling myself rising up out of myself and transcending to become part of something bigger. That's what I remember most about the protest, the feeling of excitement as I became one with the mob.**

On the flight, I was excited and terrified. First, Bob and I stopped in Detroit. The city was still burnt-out after the Detroit Uprising riots (some areas are still burnt-out to this day). It was scary. I think we also stopped in Chicago to visit a friend of his, then we arrived in Denver. Bob's sister Carolyne gave up her room for me. I felt equal parts admiration and resentment meeting the lovely Carolyne. Carolyne was slim and had long blond hair. She was studying jewelry making at art college. She was everything the lumpy seventeen-year-old me wanted to be but simply wasn't.

Bob's family took me ice skating because they thought that's what a Canadian would want to do. They were surprised that my skating ability was simply middle of the road. I suppose they

---

* I realize now that a lot of my fascination with America and Americans came from my mother, who wanted so desperately to immigrate there when she was young.

** What a dangerous feeling. It's easy to get addicted to that kind of transcendence; just think of the football hooligans in England.

imagined all Canadians were like Barbara Ann Scott. After skating, Bob's grandmother took us to Elitch's, home of the world's largest roller coaster. I knew I did not want to get on that roller coaster, or any roller coaster for that matter, but Bob's nan insisted that I would love it. I have never been so frightened in all my born days. I screamed even before it left the ground, and I have never, ever, set foot on another one of those cursed machines.

One night, Mr. and Mrs. Brownlee, Bob, and I went out to eat. Mr. Brownlee mentioned that America and Canada had been at war in 1812 and naturally America had won. I didn't have any big patriotic feelings toward Canada at that time, but it irked me that he was so sure that America had triumphed. I insisted, at the restaurant, that he was wrong, and that Canada had, in fact, won the War of 1812. I promised to prove it to him as soon as we got back. I would look it up in the encyclopedia.* The encyclopedia they had was the *Encyclopedia Americana*, which baldly stated that America had definitively won the War of 1812. I insisted that the encyclopedia was wrong and obviously had an American bias. They countered that they were right, and that Canada had lost.

I was so frustrated and felt so strongly about losing this argument. The whole experience of being far away from home, and the way things had been going so badly up to that point made it feel like the very ground was giving way beneath my feet. I was desperate to be right in at least this one thing. It's still embarrassing to remember that I actually lay down on the living room floor in Bob's parents' house in Denver, sobbing

---

* This was long, long, long before Google.

and kicking out like a three-year-old, snotting and bawling, insisting that we, the Canadians, had won the war.*

On countless occasions, *en famille*, we drove to the top of Pikes Peak. This was another terrifying experience for me. I don't like standing on the edge of anything that could be remotely called a peak. I don't want to look down. I am so afraid I'm going to fall off that I am overcome with the urge to just throw myself off and get it over with. Vertigo, I think they call it.

The first week I was in Denver I was so homesick that I threw up every morning, leading the Brownlees to assume I was knocked up. I was outraged, angry, and at the same time mortified. How dare they think that. Of course I was having sex with their son, so it was only through sheer luck, or an enormous act of will on my part, that I wasn't knocked up. I finally got my period just before Bob and I were supposed to go camping, and I made quite a show of washing the sheets. Mrs. Brownlee was visibly relieved, delighted with the news that, for now at least, I would not be the person who was carrying her first grandchild. She warned me not to go camping that week because the bears would be fatally attracted to my menstrual emissions.

I did not want to discuss my menstrual emissions, or much of anything else really, with Mrs. Brownlee. There was no love lost between us. Every morning, Mrs. Brownlee would get up at the crack of dawn and post a schedule for the day's events on the refrigerator. It read something like this:

---

* As it turns out, the War of 1812 was a draw, and if anyone could be said to have won it, it would be Britain because they managed to defend their North American colonies against the Yanks.

7:00–7:30—Get up, wash, brush teeth

7:30–8:30—Breakfast

8:30–9:00—Prepare for day's excursion

9:00–10:30—Drive to Pikes Peak

10:30–11:00—Stand on the edge of Pikes Peak and admire the view

Etc., etc.

I found her kind of scheduling and rigid preparation appalling, and I immediately took against it. (If I'm honest, I must admit that generally when I encounter anything new and unfamiliar, my first instinct is to reject it out of hand.)

One night, Bob met with his friend Chuck to rebuild Bob's old Corvette. I wanted to do something else that night and was mad that he was leaving me at home with his parents. I knew Bob had brought his dad a special bottle of Jim Bean bourbon, and I knew it was in the cupboard in the kitchen. Although I hated the taste of bourbon, I decided to have a quick drink to make myself feel better. To get to the kitchen I had to go through the living room, where Mr. and Mrs. Brownlee were jarred up on the couch watching television. I smiled at them as I sailed past. "Just getting a snack!" I yelled over my shoulder. I half-filled a tumbler with bourbon and gulped it down, and my smile was even friendlier on my way back through the living room. I lasted about twenty minutes before I decided another few gulps of bourbon would do me a world of good. I sailed past the Brownlees again. "Just feeling hungry!" I said. This time I filled the tumbler with bourbon, threw it back as fast as I could, and was a little less secure on my feet as I passed the Brownlees on my way back upstairs.

I kept going through the living room, back and forth, until the bottle was empty and I could barely walk, let alone speak. The Brownlees were horrified but did their best to be as understanding as they could.

I'm not quite sure how long I stayed with them. It might have been two weeks, or maybe even a month. Finally, Bob told me that his mother wanted me to go home and his sister wanted her room back. I didn't like them, and I certainly didn't give them any reason to like me, but I don't know if I've ever felt so deeply hurt, abandoned, and terribly ashamed. Despite all that, I said no and insisted I would not go.

The next day I did leave the Brownlee household, but I stayed in Denver an extra week or maybe two. I've kept this a shameful secret for so long that many of the details are no longer available to me. Bob put me up in some cheap motel by myself out on the highway. Bob's parents thought I was gone and Carolyne moved back into her room. The motel didn't have a restaurant, and even if it had, I didn't have much money. I do remember clearly that I was ravenously hungry (crying all day will do that to you). At that time, McDonald's hamburgers in Denver cost a dollar, and Bob would bring me one hamburger each day. As you can imagine, this did nothing to assuage my deep and abiding hunger; it just made me hungrier. (I'm suspecting now he was using my hunger as a tool that would compel me to go home.) I kept demanding three hamburgers, which I never got. Things got worse and worse, until finally—I don't remember how it happened—I got on a plane. Once I was back home, rotted out with shame and anger, I made a firm commitment to myself to never tell anyone what horrible, humiliating thing had happened to me. Once again, I had failed. Once again, I was thrown out and abandoned.

It was obvious at this point that Bob and I were not going to marry (why in the name of God would I marry someone who would only give me one hamburger a day?), but it was still what I wanted. I couldn't see any other way for my life to go forward. I was full of blind ambition. I wanted desperately to succeed at something: school, career, marrying the Yank, anything, anything at all. I wanted Bob, or anyone really, just to get out of the BigFatFailure situation I found myself in at the time. And yet, while I actively pursued everything I wanted, being perverse by nature, I also did everything in my power not to get it.

That year Aunt Mae had promised to buy me a green Triumph sports car (which cost an enormous sum of money, about $3,000) if I passed my grade eleven public exams. I badly wanted that car. But I failed my exams. I didn't even sit for a couple of them; I went to Bowring Park instead. My ability to self-sabotage knew no boundaries. I was hungry for everything, but I repeatedly did my best not to get anything.

After Denver, I didn't know what else to do except return to my old job at the Arcade, our local deep-discount store. On the public address system I made announcements like "In our men's department upstairs, from a fire sale in Montreal, men's dress shirts, only $2.99. Out they go while they last!" I was embarrassed to be working at the Arcade. Woolworths was right next door, and I longed to work there instead. "If I have to be a shop girl," I thought, "let me be a Woolworths shop girl at the very least." The Woolworths girls seemed vastly superior to us. And Woolworths itself smelled like sweet shortbread cookies, so superior to the smell of fried onions always wafting up from the snack bar at the Arcade. In the end, I didn't have the guts to quit my job at the Arcade; I just stopped going in. It took me six or seven years after that to get up the courage to walk through the doors as a customer.

I wanted so much for myself and had such vaunting ambition, but I didn't know exactly what it was I wanted, other than success, any form of success. Underneath all that, I now understand that what I wanted was to *be* wanted, to be a part of and not apart from. I can see now that I didn't want to marry Bob, which would have been disastrous. And thanks be to God I didn't get that Triumph. Drinking and driving was much more common in those days, and the only time I ever got the urge to drive was when I was right on the verge of going into a blackout. Luckily for me and the entire population of Newfoundland, I didn't have anything to drive until I was forty-nine and had been clean and sober for nine years.

Bob, I think, went on to study computer science at Boulder University. I can't say for certain because I cut off all communication with him, though I'm pretty sure I kept telling Aunt Mae and all my friends that we were still engaged. Back then, when things went wrong I just cut out of the situation and never looked back. When I returned to St. John's after that trip, I felt hopeless. After I quit the Arcade I would lie on the couch in the front room all day and watch CBC TV. We only had two stations at that time and *Coronation Street* was my favourite show. Aunt Mae would sometimes poke her head around the doorframe and in the mildest way possible inquire if I was okay, and did I think maybe I should see Dr. O'Brien, the psychiatrist. She always said Dr. O'Brien sotto voce—the idea that your life could be so wrecked that you might want to see a psychiatrist was surely something that shouldn't be spoken about above a whisper. Aunt Mae was very worried about me, and so was I.

But one afternoon, lying on the couch feeling very low-minded watching *Coronation Street*, there was a public service announcement that the CBC was looking for someone to do an on-air summer replacement job for a morning show called *Summer Magazine*. I could barely lift my head off the cushion, but I thought, "I have been on the PA system at the Arcade, and the CBC Radio building is just across the street, so . . ." I can't really imagine what I was thinking, but for some reason I hauled myself up off the couch, and the next day I went down to audition. I was so sure that I would never get the job, and so deeply in despair, that I lacked the energy needed to be nervous or anxious. Because of this, I came across in the audition as relaxed, confident, and announcer-like. I got the job.

I was terrible at it. The only mail we ever got was a letter from a gentleman in Grand Falls who wrote to ask the identity of the mad giggler who was on the air from ten o'clock to eleven. And I seemed to get right up on the last nerve of the producer of *Summer Magazine*, John Fleet—"Fleet as in street, not as in enema," as everyone in the radio building would say whenever they mentioned his name.

Later in life, I did settle into a long-term relationship with an American. My son Jess's father is a Yank. An actual real Connecticut Yank. Ray was and is one of the sweetest men on the planet, but with a wicked sense of humour. When we were together, he compulsively teased and tantalized and baited me until he got a rise out of me or made me lose my cool. Thirty years ago, it didn't take much baiting to make me lose my cool and launch into a red rage, or collapse in a spell of violent weeping. I'm not sure that was exactly the response Ray was looking for. But our families are very close friends now. And like all the piled-up disasters of my early years, it has worked out for the best. It's taken me thirty years of sobriety to realize it, but the old adage "It'll all work out in the end, and if it doesn't work out, it's not the end" does seem to be true. Of course, there are some things I won't ever get to see the end of, and maybe that's just as well.

Write What You Know

AT A PARTY LAST YEAR, THE AWARD-WINNING AUTHOR Lisa Moore took me aside and said she thought I had been very brave to write about bad sex in my first and only novel, *Crying for the Moon*. Her remark reminded me of the advice that is so often given to young writers: "Write what you know." And certainly, in terms of sex, bad is what I knew best.

It all started out quite badly for me. I was eight or nine, and there was an old man who lived out the road from our country shack. He was so old that he'd been involved in the Great Newfoundland Sealing Disaster of 1914,* but he made it home, having miraculously survived two days trapped on an ice floe in a vicious blizzard, while all about him his shipmates were dying, frozen

---

* On March 31, 1914, 132 men were ordered onto the North Atlantic ice floes to hunt seals, but only fifty-four made it back alive.

into macabre shapes.* Somehow he managed to live through all that.

I was delighted with his attention when I first met him. At that time I lived with my two maiden aunts and my uncle. I very rarely saw my dad, and Uncle Jack was the only constant male figure in my life. Uncle Jack had already had nine strokes and a blood clot through his brain, and so he spent most of his time with his chin on his chest, his paralyzed arm resting on his paralyzed leg, and generally being deeply depressed.** My friend, the sealing disaster survivor, was hale and hearty. He would take me for walks in the road to the pond or out to the shop. Me and a lot of other kids would watch this man's TV through his window. When a crowd of us gathered round, he'd turn up the sound so we could hear it. None of us kids had TVs at that point.

One evening, he invited me inside to watch TV, and I felt so special to be allowed in. I didn't even get a chance to sit down before he put his hand down the waistband of my summer shorts and proceeded to touch me in such a way that I knew something bad was happening. The terrible thing, the thing that made me feel the most guilt-ridden and the thing that really marked me, I believe, was the fact that as well as deep mortification and terror, I also felt a certain amount of pleasure. The pleasure I felt made me know that I was a very, very bad person, a very bad girl indeed. I ran home, and all that

---

* When the dead were brought back to St. John's on the *Bellaventure*, they were still frozen. Men were frozen into grotesque, ice-bound sculptures, horrifying icy figures of brothers holding brothers, men huddled together trying to stay alive.

** But Uncle Jack was kind for all that.

night as I lay wide awake in my bunk bed, I burned with shame, confusion, guilt, remorse. I took it on as my sin because I had felt that lewd pleasure. My little eight-year-old Catholic brain somehow believed that the fault was mine. I just felt so dirty inside. I didn't tell anyone for years—partly, I think, because it just happened that one time and I had not been physically brutalized in any way. In fact, the horror of the whole situation for me was that lewd pleasure. I made a pact with myself that night that I would never let myself feel that awful, degrading, shameful pleasure again. And until I was in my fifties, I didn't. For many, many years I dismissed the whole incident as nothing, just my alarmist self once again making a trauma mountain out of a one-off molehill.

It's remarkable, isn't it, how strong and lasting the promises you make to yourself when you're eight can be.

It was deeply shaming the next time, too. I was again the sinner, or so I thought. I was sixteen and hosting a Christmas party. Aunt Mae had said she'd go upstairs to Mrs. Malone's apartment, and I could have a real grown-up, unsupervised party. I remember I wore a short, short silver shirtdress that I was so proud of, and matching silver shoes. I drank about, I'd say, three-quarters of a bottle of Old Niagara sherry—or Pinkie as the winos of downtown St. John's called it.* I had an all-consuming crush on a boy who I don't think was that fond of me, but I was determined that he would be mine. Like I said, I was drunk, and it was just turning to 1969. The Summer of Love had come and gone, and there I was, still a virgin.

---

* It had the reputation of not only being the cheapest but also having the highest alcohol content.

I didn't want to be that uptight, that non-groovy, that not with it.

I said out loud for all the party to hear that I wanted to have sex with that boy; actually, I said I wanted to fuck that boy. That's the last thing I remember until I came to in the back seat of a Volkswagen, my silver dress and the seat of the Volkswagen covered in blood, me and that boy in the back, and to my horror, the boyfriend of a friend of mine driving behind the wheel. The driver was very upset; it was his father's car and he didn't know how he was going to get the blood out of the upholstery in the back seat. It was a real-life case of a girl in a short, short dress just asking for it, or that's the way I saw it at the time and for years after.

My little brother Greg was back at the party (he was staying with Aunt Mae and me for the weekend). I remember him being very concerned, and despite how upset I was, I felt very touched by his concern. I couldn't stop crying, but my friends Tralee, Ester, and Pat—the three musketeers—took me into the bathroom, mopped up my tears, and basically said, "It's about fuckin' time. We were wondering if and when it was ever gonna happen to you."

The first time I had sex when I wasn't drunk or underage was at the Welcome Hotel with that American serviceman I was determined to marry. It was dreadful, but mercifully short. I believed for the longest time—and truthfully this belief still lingers sometimes—that if you had sex with no foreplay, and there was then no pleasure whatsoever involved, the sin of sex was already paid for and you might "get away with it." In other words, I was sinning by having sex, but at the same time, having sex was the punishment in and of itself.

Then there was the terrible, awful, relentless sex I had with the first man I ever lived with. I was eighteen, and we moved in together even though he had already been violent toward me as well as emotionally abusive. Ironically, all the time I was being physically and psychologically abused by him, I was attending those wonderful '70s feminist consciousness-raising groups. They were great. I was deeply committed to second-stage feminism, although I was finding it very difficult to live by its principles. The women in my consciousness-raising groups would talk about how important it was to have satisfying sex with your partner, and how necessary it was to talk to him about your sexual needs and desires.*

I eventually listened to this advice, and against my better judgement, decided to take it. I approached talking to my rageful and physically violent partner** with great trepidation.*** We were in bed, having just had another session of horrible sex, and I was speaking to his awful, pimply back. As usual, he had quickly turned over after he came so he could fall asleep immediately. I said in a small non-upsetting (or so I thought) voice, "Umm, you know, I've never really ever had an orgasm. I mean . . ." I quickly added, "I mean ever. I mean long, long, long before I ever met you, I never had an orgasm." He turned toward me with alarming speed and fixed me with his most murderous gaze. My remark had filled him with anger and even

---

* They would often debate the relative merits of vaginal and clitoral orgasm. I thought it was all bullshit.

** I once actually saw this guy dancing with rage, totally naked, screaming, face purple, his sausage and his two scotch eggs flipping and flopping about wildly. If I hadn't been so afraid of him, I would have laughed uncontrollably at that ludicrous sight.

***He had thrown me over the stairs, bitten my ear through, and torn out a lot of the hair on the left side of my head, and that was just the first time he was violent toward me. And by this time, things had gotten way worse.

worse, as it turned out, a determination to bring me to orgasm come hell or high water. To him that meant banging away at me hour after hour (or that's how long it seemed, anyway) in the persistent and punishing way that, for him, passed for sexual intimacy.

It was so boring and so painful, and on top of that I thought, "Oh, now I'm really screwed," *pardon the pun*, because I couldn't any longer quickly bring the misery to an end by faking my regular, phony orgasm. He was young and seemed to have an inexhaustible ability to keep at it. Finally, I was forced to put all my acting skills into play. I moaned and I panted with a whole new fervor and an even higher degree of phony passion in a herculean effort to bring my suffering to an end. Miraculously, he bought it, and at least the dreadful sex didn't have to last so long.*

I don't mind confessing that I am part of that fake orgasm generation. All that phony heavy breathing, all that bogus steamy ardor—what a performance, what a big fat lie. Even after I finally escaped from Mr. Angry** and all his frenzied fury I stayed at the fake orgasm business. Sometimes I went too far. I remember one fella pulling back, wondering if I was okay. What was wrong with me? Did I have the flu or pneumonia or something? My breathing was so loud and erratic. Of course, he didn't wait for an answer. He just went right back at it, grinding away at me at an ever-increasing speed. He

---

* This was prior to Meg Ryan's amazing job faking an orgasm in *When Harry Met Sally*.

** And yet it took me forever to leave him. I did try to poison him once; that's another story. It took years for me to get out of that horrific situation.

was obviously concerned that with the kind of laboured heavy breathing I was doing I might not be long for this world, so it was even more essential for him to get his rocks off as quickly as possible.

It was exhausting though, all that tiresome laboured breathing, sometimes to the point where I'd almost hyperventilate, and the moaning and the groaning and the panting, and the *Oh Gods* and the *Jesus in the garden*, all that phony fervor—I mean my mouth would be so dry by the end of it, let alone my down below bits. But they'd just keep banging away and that was genuinely terrifying. Think about it: all that friction, coupled with the deep desert-like dryness down below. It's a miracle that I didn't just burst into flames every time I went at it.

"Live horse, and you'll get water," Aunt Mae always said. And it took me living until I was in my fifties to get there. It's terrifically embarrassing to admit this when everyone else who writes a memoir seems to be able to come on a dime. Yes, I was in my fifties before I ever had an orgasm. I always thought the talk of the female orgasm was just more bullshit. But when it finally happened to me, I was floored. Suddenly I was in a fever of desire, and I became as relentless as one of those young men I'd wrestled with in my youth. I remember having to rush into the bathroom to masturbate while I was waiting to see my GP, or if I was at the emergency room or even waiting in the dentist's office, and quickly, and not to brag, efficiently, bring myself to orgasm. On the plane, I couldn't make it from St. John's to Halifax without retiring to the tiny bathroom at the back. My husband and I were shocking. Summer or winter. We'd take off into the woods, on a hike to Gros Morne, or fall deliriously into a hidden snowbank. I was in love with my husband, Don. And I was besotted with sex. At some point though, everything changed and orgasms (which I'm grateful to have experienced, at least for a few years) became very painful. I tried to keep at it, hoping things would change (they didn't). It's not common post-menopausal vaginal dryness—if only it were. I've seen psychologists, gynecologists, physical therapists, you name 'em. No one can diagnose the problem. So as gloriously and happily as I suddenly started having orgasms (shout out to my wonderful husband), I stopped. Endless research has shown that victims/survivors of childhood sexual abuse often experience sexual dysfunction (as well as a whole host of other physical and psychological problems).

Remember that when I was growing up, sex was a very dangerous pursuit for women. I believe that even had I not been molested, satisfying sex would perhaps always have been difficult, if not impossible. I saw the price my sisters paid: teenage pregnancies, financial instability, violent relationships, and a host of related problems. Every time my sisters had sex, it seemed they brought forth another child. My upstairs guardians never stopped being outraged or referring to the fact that my mother bore two children who were not my father's. Sin, sexual sin, was massive in Irish Catholicism. It was drilled into us that sex was only for procreation within the strict confines of a Catholic marriage. Everything to do with sex, even French-kissing, was a one-way ticket to the fiery pit of Hell. To paraphrase the great George Carlin, it was a mortal sin to want to have sex, another mortal sin to think about having sex, and a third sin if you planned to have sex. So even without any physical contact, you'd already committed three mortal sins and were well on your way to face an eternity of torture in the arms of Abaddon, dark angel of the abyss.

Sadly, I have spent the better part of a lifetime haunted by the dark shadows of what I learned as a child.

Codco

It was the best of times, it was the worst of times.
—Charles Dickens

The beauty of the world . . . has two edges, one of laughter, one of anguish, cutting the heart asunder.
—Virginia Woolf

There are two kinds of comedians, diagnosed and undiagnosed.
—Mike MacDonald (brilliant Canadian comedian)

CODCO.* IT WAS 1973, AND WHEN WE WEREN'T LAUGHing, we were fighting (and we fought and laughed a lot). We were all young. I think Tommy Sexton was only fifteen then, I was twenty, Cathy Jones was seventeen. Andy Jones and Greg

---

* When the members of the Codco Comedy Troupe were growing up, cod was everything. When you acted up as a child, your mother called you a "cod of misery." When you behaved like a fool, people said you were "codding around." So choosing to call ourselves Cod Company, or Codco for short, seemed inevitable.

Malone were the senior members at twenty-four, Dyan Olsen and Paul Sametz were twenty, and Bob Joy was twenty-three. Most of us had grown up in some sort of dysfunctional home, and of course we brought all that dysfunction to the table. We didn't know any better. I didn't, anyway.

I have so many conflicting views and mad emotions that I find it difficult to bring any kind of clarity, let alone precision and factuality, to writing about my time in Codco. Over the years, working with other companies has proven to be much simpler and easier. In those other companies, we didn't live as deeply in each other's pockets, the way we did in Codco. Codco was a 24-hour-a-day job, and not really a job as much as a whole life. We were colleagues, and lovers, and haters, and brothers and sisters, and best friends for life; we tried to be everything to each other. I don't know what anyone else from Codco would say if they were writing this essay, but for me those years were a long, arduous, and heartbreaking experience, yet at the same time so wonderful, so exciting, and such a vital period of growth. I learned so much about comedy, about theatre, about how to work with other people without losing your mind. In Codco, I finally got some sense of who I might be.

Once in the early to mid-'70s, before Codco was a TV show, when we still called ourselves a theatre company, I was at a party, locked in the bathroom.* There I was, lacking any sense of self-worth or even any sense of self,** feeling like an outsider, lost and alone, when I overheard two people outside the bath-

---

* God, I always hated parties—still do, really.
** It surprised me when I was in recovery to learn that feeling bad about yourself was still totally self-centred behaviour.

room door talking about Codco, saying how funny it was and how culturally important it was for Newfoundland at that time. The party was being held at an academic's house, and while I don't remember exactly who the two speakers were, I think they were professors at Memorial University. I do remember clearly, however, sitting on the toilet and feeling, maybe for the first time in my life, that at last I might be *something*, or at least be a *part of something*. And it was a *something* that other people thought was important.* I was always driven by ambition, wanting to be somebody, but I really had no idea who that somebody might be. Up to that point I hadn't garnered any pleasure or satisfaction from my acting or my writing—or from very much else, really—but I recall that on that night, for a few hours at least, I felt that I was something. And that I was something because I was part of the larger entity called Codco.

IN THE BEGINNING

When I was just eighteen years old and busy doing a dreadful job hosting *Summer Magazine* on CBC Radio,** Dudley Cox and David Wiser, part of the St. John's amateur theatre scene, were starting a new theatre company. Dudley Cox heard me on the radio, liked my voice, and thought I'd do a great job playing the queen in a piece he'd just written called *Sing a Song of Sixpence*, based on the nursery rhyme of the same name. Dudley asked me to take part in the play, and because I had no

---

* This, I think, was the beginning of my workaholism.
** See "Makin' Time with the Yanks."

impulse control and no ability to say no,* I agreed. In Dudley's version, the king was in the counting house counting out his money and I, playing the queen, was in my parlour orgasmically eating bread and honey. This part was extremely difficult for me to get a handle on. Having never had an orgasm, I didn't know how to act my way through one.** But one thing I knew for sure: I did not want to pretend to have an orgasm on stage in the basement of the Arts and Culture Centre in front of fifty or so people.***

I was so bad at playing the orgasmic queen that Dudley insisted on re-rehearsing it every day before the performance, but no matter how much we rehearsed, I just could never do it. I could not let go in that way. Not even in the bedroom, let alone on stage. Despite my deep discomfort with being on stage, I carried on acting, but never really finding the courage to let go. I liked being in amateur theatre because of the camaraderie and the drinking (mostly the drinking, I think). There were always so many parties, so many reasons to drink, to escape.

While in no way a success for me, *Sing a Song of Sixpence* did open the door to my acting career, a career which, at that time, I didn't really want or feel I was any good at. It was the start of it all, my first introduction to life in the theatre, and despite my failure and my extreme reservations and discomfort, I, too, became an "Arts and Culture Centre Rat" (the name Tommy Sexton's father always called him). I went on that year

---

* This is still a bit of a struggle for me.

** Meg Ryan hadn't had her completely convincing orgasm in *When Harry Met Sally* yet, and I hadn't come up with my phony breathing routine yet either. Like a female frog, I thought if I just lay there, like I was dead, they might knock it off.

***I was deeply sexually repressed, and now believe if it wasn't for copious amounts of liquor, God alone knows if I ever would have had sex.

to perform in many amateur productions as well as the Provincial and Dominion drama festivals. And that summer, for the grand sum of $40 a week, I had my first professional theatrical engagement.

Dudley and David started a new, semi-professional, touring company called the Newfoundland Travelling Theatre Company. In 1971 we did a massive tour, winding our way through the Coves and Tickles, the Harbours and the Bights, and the Arms and the Heads and the Barachois of the province. We slept in cots on gym floors in schools across the island. Every night, save Mondays, we played a British farce called *See How They Run*, and every morning we did *The Wizard of Oz* for the youngsters. That summer was the first time I worked with most of the people who'd later become Codco.

It was the first time I met and worked with Andy Jones, Dyan Olsen, and Bob Joy, although I'd gone through grade school with Andy's sister Mary-Wynn, and Bob's family always sat in the pew in front of us at 10:15 mass. I'd worked with Tommy Sexton extensively the year before, and his older brother Marty had been in our grade eight gang. In that insular Newfoundland way, although we were strangers we also knew each other deeply, almost generationally. My mom was from the Harbour Main district, and Bob's father was the member of the House of Assembly for Harbour Main. Andy's uncle was the priest in Mom's church in Conception, and Andy's father and his uncle Andrew would sometimes perform in Christmas concerts at the parish hall in Conception Harbour. My mother was deeply taken with them and thought they were the funniest couple of fellas she ever saw. Forty years later, I felt the same way about Andy. His sister Cathy and

Greg Malone did the fall tour with the Newfoundland Theatre Company. Greg's brother Kerry was the cutest guy in our grade eight gang. I had another familial connection with Greg: his grandfather sold musical instruments, and back in the day my nan had bought a rosewood Victrola from him. This was a very big-ticket item for Nan and her family, and people talked about it with a certain amount of awe, even in my day. In fact, when I was growing up that Victrola still held pride of place in the living room.

Despite not really knowing each other, we were somehow all connected through our families and our churches and our schools, etc. (God knows we might have all been distantly related in that particularly cozy Newfoundland way.)

Dyan Olsen was the exotic member of the troop. She had blond hair and beautiful blue eyes, and her parents weren't even from Newfoundland; they were from the Prairies. Her father was a professor of agriculture at Memorial University and had developed the Pink Pearl potato, which was resistant to the dreadful Newfoundland potato blight.

We had such an adventure on that summer tour and on the subsequent fall outing. We all fell in love with each other, with theatre, and with Newfoundland. We performed at least two shows a day. At night I played Penelope, the vicar's wife, the straight man, and the most boring character in *See How They Run*. Every morning I played the Wicked Witch of the West. I didn't want to be the Wicked Witch of the West; I longed to be Glinda, the good witch. (I am aware that the Wicked Witch is probably a more interesting role, but as I think I may have mentioned previously in these essays, I have never wanted what I have, and I have always longed for what I don't.)*

It was an extraordinary time, taking us into some communities that had only recently been made accessible by road. We drove on dirt roads, right from the tip of the province, down to the bottom of its southern boot. We played in isolated communities that had never, other than local concerts, seen live theatre. During *The Wizard of Oz* in some of the more remote communities, children would scream in terror when Dorothy and Toto the dog came on stage. But those same children, when I came through the audience in my witch's hat and cloak, those same terrified children who had been made weak by the sight of Dorothy and her darling dog Toto, would step up to me, fists clenched, and challenge me outside. They would step on my cloak and threaten to "beat the bearings out of me." They recognized me as the bad one, and these plucky youngsters from places like St. Lawrence and other distant communities saw it as their job to take me on, put me in my place, and courageously defeat evil.

While we were touring the province, I was still in a brutally abusive relationship, and because St. John's was a small town, everyone knew it. One day, as the full company was on its way to another show, we were driving down a steep, steep hill on the Northern Peninsula. The sun was splittin' the rocks, and I was feeling particularly buoyant, (I could have been coming off as a bit cocky I guess) when one of the actors said to me that I was the type who deserved a good smack in

---

* Try to avoid this as a way of life if you can. There is no satisfaction in it.

the mouth, or a beating, I can't remember his exact words now, but I was shattered, because, of course, I always believed that was the truth—that the beatings were my fault and I deserved them. But to hear it said aloud, and to think that someone else thought something as bad about me as I did about myself, it really knocked me down. There were lots of times that summer that were not so good; but then again, there were times that were glorious. I remember Andy Jones reading aloud to us from various plays as we drove from venue to venue, and it made the endless hours fly by. The one that struck me the most was a play called *The Ruling Class*. They made it into a movie starring Peter O'Toole, but seeing the movie was not nearly as good as listening to Andy read the lines to us as we drove down the Burin Peninsula.

During those early years on stage I always felt afraid of the audience, terrified they didn't like me and could see that I was no good and a fraud. My response to this was to spend most of my stage energy trying to reassure the audience that I didn't think I was any good either, trying to prove to them that I was on their side. I was desperate not to appear a fool and get caught out thinking "too much of myself."* Thanks to Andy Jones's help, on that tour, bit by bit I began to feel more comfortable on stage—just a little; I still wasn't mad about the stage work, but I loved the travelling troupe aspect of that summer, rolling into town like sailors coming into a new port, anonymous and free. No one knew us, and those were the days I felt the most footloose and closest to being my real self.

---

* Funny, isn't it? Most of the time I was on stage I was being called upon to "play the fool."

I haven't even started talking about Codco yet and here I am, caught up in the weeds with a lengthy story of how we all got together. In my defense, I think it's important. There was some magic afoot in that beginning. It was the start of a professional life for so many of us, and for me it was the first faint beginnings of having a life. Or at least having a life I might consider worth living.

But even then, I wasn't happy with what I had. Secretly, I wanted to be a journalist. But because I was on the pip all the way through high school, I didn't have the necessary marks to get into Carleton or some other journalism school. I got into the theatre program at Ryerson by the skin of my teeth. I was so full of shame and fear that while I was trying to perform the classical piece for the audition, faculty members had to come on stage and hold my hand the whole way through Katherina's monologue in *The Taming of the Shrew*. To this day, I still don't know how in the name of God I managed to get in.

It was 1973. I started at Ryerson. Greg Malone moved to Toronto to be part of Theatre Passe Muraille. Tommy finished grade ten at Brother Rice and hitchhiked to Toronto to find work in the theatre. Cathy, Dyan, Paul Sametz (whom I'd worked with in the Mummers Troupe), and I got an apartment together on Huron Street. Coming to Toronto in the early '70s was no easy task. Newfoundlanders were still the butt of every mainland joke, still the "goofy Newfie" too stunned to do anything right.* This enraged us but at the same time we felt deeply ashamed. Joey Smallwood had said he'd hauled Newfoundland

---

* At that time Quebec had a small publishing industry based entirely on Newfie joke books.

kicking and screaming out of the nineteenth century and into the twentieth. But even if he did, we still felt behind the times and out of step with the rest of the country—and the rest of the country did their best to encourage that feeling.

At some point that year, Dyan and Tommy auditioned for Paul Thompson, the grandfather of Canadian Collective Theatre. They wanted to take part in a soon-to-be-written show called Under the Graywacke (Greg Malone actually did that show). Thompson of course saw Tommy and Dyan's obvious talent, generously gave them $300, and told them they should do a show of their own. With that money, and using some of our aforementioned rage—and desperate to put the shame behind us—that's just what we did. Thompson offered us space for rehearsal and a performance venue—a church with a soup kitchen—on Sherbourne Street near Moss Park and Allan Gardens.

Tommy and Dyan basically formed Codco when they asked all their housemates and Greg Malone to join them in writing a show about Newfoundland that would make fun of the way Newfoundland was seen by the rest of the country. Together we wrote a comedy called *Cod on a Stick*. We played at the Sherbourne soup kitchen for a one-week run. The show received wonderful notices from Toronto critics and was held over for an extra two weeks. Andy Jones and Bob Joy were not part of that original show. Andy was in Europe touring with the Ken Campbell Road Show, and Bob was Rhodes Scholaring at Oxford, but with Andy's permission we did use a couple of comedy pieces he'd written. Pieces that had made us pee in our pants with laughter during that glorious summer tour, including "Hello Mrs. Prichard, Alfred's Dead," a dark piece of comic genius featuring a blind man and his heartbroken mother. We wrote songs, too. One was based entirely on graffiti I saw on a toilet stall at the Imperial Tavern: "The cod fish lie dead in the ocean, the cod fish lie dead in the sea, they all died of water pollution caused by the oil industry." We changed "cod fish" to "wild cod," which seemed sillier and funnier in a way. The notion that there would be no cod in Newfoundland—Newfoundland, where the cod were famously so thick in the water people could just dip a basket in the sea and pull up cod fish in their teeming thousands—was inconceivable in 1973. Of course, once again life imitating art, by 1992 the wild cod did indeed lie dead in the ocean.

To write *Cod on a Stick* we used stories we'd heard, things we'd lived through. We used our parents' stories, things that happened to our brothers and sisters. And on top of that, we used all the bottled-up anger we felt at being dismissed as "goofy Newfies," always considered to be "less than" by our Canadian compatriots.* We used everything that we had.

When I was at the CBC the previous summer, broadcaster Dave Gunn often told a story about interviewing a lighthouse keeper from a remote part of Newfoundland who was very, very taciturn. No matter what question Dave asked, he would only reply "yes" or "no." Dave got desperate, but thought he had the man when he asked how the whole complex operation of the lighthouse worked. Much to Dave's chagrin, the lighthouse

---

* At that time, the major question for Canadians was "Who are we?" We had no trouble answering that question. We knew who Canadians were. They were the crowd that thought they were so much better than us.

keeper simply replied "pullies." This became a very popular sketch in the show. Tommy played the lighthouse keeper.

Dyan and Paul had worked with the Mummers Theatre Troupe and had done a sketch called "Mother England" and "Newfie Puppet." We took these characters and wrote a new sketch. Tommy's parents, Sara and Ned, were the opening two characters of the show. Mary White, Greg's wife, told a story about an around-the-bay taxi ride involving a blind man and a cruelly insensitive passenger, which opened up to include Tommy's uncle's story, my sister's best friend's experience with cancer, and then all of our experiences riding in around-the-bay taxis in the '60s and '70s. The taxis were built to accommodate six passengers, seven at the most, but often transported twelve, sometimes even fourteen people, into St. John's.

I remember staying up late with Cathy Jones in the kitchen on Huron Street, writing small pieces that would tie the different sketches together. We imagined ourselves to be a company called "Bridges Incorporated." By two or three in the morning, we were weak with laughter. Sometimes when Cathy and I worked together it was unbelievably fun and funny. But during most of our time together, Cathy and I had great difficulty. It was hard on both of us. We were so much alike. We looked alike, we were just about the same height, we played the same type of characters, and everybody called Cathy Mary, and me Cathy, which when we were young broke our hearts and made us feel completely unseen.

As we got older, Cathy didn't mind it so much when people thought she was Marg, Princess Warrior, and it didn't bother me at all when people gave me big props for the brilliant "Angry Yoga" sketch that Cathy did.*

BACK TO THE SHOW

We opened with the song "Cod on a Stick."** Our plan was to carry sweet little red-and-white striped sticks topped with real cod heads. We went to Kensington Market to look for them, but cod heads were totally unavailable in downtown Toronto at the time. So we bought ourselves six Bighead Carp heads to put on the ends of our stripey sticks. As we came on stage singing our up-tempo opening song, bits and bobs of slimy carp brains dripped alarmingly down our arms. It was an unprepossessing beginning, quite horrifying for us and for the audience, too, I might add. We always blamed it on being in Ontario, where

---

* Long after Codco, even after I'd left *This Hour Has 22 Minutes*, Cathy did an ad for a drug to combat vaginal dryness. There was an uproar in the press, and people were outraged that pharmaceutical companies were once again making a normal condition of the aging female body into a medical issue. That didn't bother Cathy at all. What upset her was the thought that people might mistakenly believe she suffered from the condition. She said for once she didn't mind at all that people were mistaking us, thinking she was Marg, Princess Warrior, and I was the one with the dried-up old cunt. We laughed a lot over that.

** "Oh, you think that we're so funny,
just a cod on a stick. You think that we're hilarious,
a seal in an aquarious,
but b'ys you must be awful tick.
We're takin' over, we're movin' up here.
Fish and Brewis and fillets,
and all our fishin' gear.
Oh the plane in millions,
flyin' through the sky,
Super Newf and all his troops to spit into your eye."

we were reduced to using crappy old Bighead Carp heads, but really, cod heads may well have been just as disgusting. In the end, we went with little construction paper cutouts of cod heads.

The day before we intended to reopen for our holdover, I was called into the dean of theatre's office at Ryerson and told I would have to quit Codco because it was the policy of Ryerson's theatre department that students could not work in the theatre and continue to study theatre. The dean feared we might pick up a lot of bad habits if we worked in the actual theatre.

So I quit Codco and got a job at a somewhat infamous bar on Yonge Street called the Coq d'Or.* There were a lot of rules at the Coq d'Or. As a waitress, I was not allowed to serve any customer wearing a hat. It was 1973, and a lot of Coq d'Or's clientele wore what we then affectionately called "pimp hats,"** and I would have to, as politely as I could, insist that those hats be removed. The system at the Coq d'Or was that I would come in every night with $20 of my own money, and pay the bar for whatever drinks my customers had ordered, then the customer would pay me. I was required to carry $18 in paper money wrapped around my middle finger, and $2 worth of change in the ashtray of my serving tray. When a customer ordered a drink, I took their order to the bar and paid for it, hoping and praying that said customer wouldn't be angry with me for asking him to remove his pimp hat and wouldn't stiff me for the drink.

One night a pimp-hat-wearing table ordered four whiskey

---

* Sheia Rogers also worked there when she was going to university.
** Apparently they're still called pimp hats to this day, but you saw a lot more of them in 1973/1974.

sours. After I paid for the drinks and brought them to their table, I discovered they'd all left. That same night, someone stole the $2 change from my ashtray, so not only did I not make any money that night, I went home $20 poorer than I'd come in. And I'd had to borrow that $20 in the first place. Also, "Midnight Train to Georgia" was playing a lot, and I could not stop sobbing along to it. I think that was night four of my waitressing career. It proved to be my last. I was a terrible waitress, even a worse waitress than I was an actress. So I went back to Codco, left Ryerson, and we all headed home to do a two-month tour of *Cod on a Stick* throughout Newfoundland. Bob Joy joined the company, replacing Paul Sametz,* and Andy came back from England and the Ken Campbell Road Show.

The tour of Newfoundland and our shows in St. John's proved to be a roaring success. Andy suggested that if we stayed home we could make St. John's the theatrical centre of North America. (Of course I know we didn't achieve that, but neither did Columbus get to India. He did, however, get somewhere, and so did we.) I stayed; by that time I would have been delighted to be anywhere Andy Jones was. Greg stayed. Dyan and Tommy were developing dreadlocks and had adopted a Rastafarian way of life and a vegan diet. Cathy and Bob were also drifting toward Rastafarianism. Andy and I stood firm against it.

Codco's second show was called *Sickness, Death, and Beyond the Grave*. The title celebrated what we thought, or rather

---

* Bob Joy's mother never forgave us. Bob was a Rhodes Scholar and was on his summer break from Oxford when he joined the company. The tour was longer than expected so Bob asked for an extension on his break; his college, Christchurch, wouldn't give it to him. He decided to quit Oxford and stay with Codco. Mrs. Joy never really got over it.

knew, to be the three big topics of conversation in Newfoundland at the time. (For some reason, we left out weather, which continues to this day, along with sickness and death, to dominate Newfoundlanders' communication.) So Cathy Jones, Andy Jones, Bob Joy, Greg Malone, Dyan Olsen, Tommy Sexton, and I became the official company called Codco. Our writing process went something like this: we'd sit around and talk every morning, and somehow or other, one of the stories we told—about our childhood, or something that happened to us on the way to rehearsal that morning, or what we had been fighting about with our significant other—something inevitably caught the collective imagination. We'd get to our feet and start improvising around that theme. We'd tape the improvisation, then usually we would improvise maybe two, maybe ten more times. Then someone would listen to and transcribe the tapes and pick out the funniest material, and we'd cobble together a script. Or sometimes people brought in a sketch that was already crafted and we'd all try to elbow our way into that piece of work.

Andy Jones and I were looking to rent an apartment together. We had very little money and we wanted to live downtown. We found a lovely third-story apartment on Prescott Street, roomy and cheap. But as we were viewing it we noticed a room with a locked door. When we asked the landlady what that room was for, she said, "Oh that's where I sleeps." *In our apartment?!* "Oh yes," she said, implying by her look that she wasn't foolish enough to let strangers be up on her third floor on their own. *God alone knows what they might get up to.* We told that story at the Codco rehearsal the next day, and out of those thin beginnings grew "The House of Budgell," a long-running sketch in which Greg Malone and I played Eustace and Dulcie

Budgell, the rapacious landlords of a downtown St. John's boarding house.

For *Sickness, Death, and Beyond the Grave*, of course, we needed a coffin. We went to a funeral home, and much to our surprise, they loaned us one. It was what was called at the time a *welfare coffin*. It was fiberboard covered with grey cloth, and it was perfect for our needs. The funeral director could not have been nicer or more generous. Still, we all drew back in alarm when he opened the coffin. He looked at us and laughed. "There's nothing to be scared of with a coffin," he told us. "It's like a sausage: it's nothin' till the meat goes in."

We took *Sickness, Death, and Beyond the Grave* to Toronto and around Ontario. We may have gone west, too, but I don't remember now. I do know that everywhere we went we were regaled with stories of sickness and death, and spooky happenings from beyond the grave.

Our next show was called *Old Material to Prove to the Unemployment Insurance People That We Definitely Weren't Working When We Said We Weren't*. After that, we did *Das Capital, or What Do You Want to See the Harbour for, Anyway?* It was a show protesting city plans that would destroy downtown St. John's and put a four-lane highway right through the centre of it. Those plans also included the building of unending numbers of tumbling towers to perch on the waterfront, effectively cutting the citizens of St. John's off from their harbour, and the narrows, and the very reasons that anyone would have settled in St. John's in the first place. A lot of those plans to destroy the City of St. John's were stymied by the fact that the city had no money. At the time, being broke was seen as a bad thing, but it saved us from turning into poor Saint John, New

Brunswick, where the Trans-Canada Highway runs right through its downtown.* Next, we did an Ontario tour called *Hot on Ice with Figgy Duff*, then *Would You Like to Smell My Pocket Crumbs?* and finally *The Tale Ends*, our last theatrical show as a troupe.

Everything I write about Codco is made up of fragments and feelings, but some things stand out in broad relief. For instance, I can tell you about the time in 1976 when as part of Canada's cultural gift to America to help her celebrate her Bicentennial, we played the Walnut Street Theatre in Philadelphia for a week. We received great applause and sterling reviews. The most exciting thing, however, was that the Newfoundland Club of Philadelphia bought out our last night's performance and were having a reception for us after the show. I remember feeling jubilant but at the same time a little apprehensive. My brother Mike, or Big Mick, as he was known in his heyday, was married and living in Philadelphia. An ironworker, he had all the attributes of that hardworking, hard-drinking, extraordinarily heroic group that often boasted they built New York . . . and Philadelphia . . . and Chicago, etc.

I wasn't sure how Mike and his crowd would feel about the Codco show. My apprehension was warranted. The Newfoundland Club was outraged. People yelled out from the audience, "Why don't you show the progress? All the new roads?" When Father Dinn, Andy's hilarious hellfire and brimstone Redemptorist Priest, said he was going to "go now, boys and girls, and jump off the wharf," many members of the

---

* It's so often the case that things that appear dreadful in the moment can turn out to be a blessing in the end.

Newfoundland Club in the audience yelled, "So you should, my son! So should ye all." Like every other expatriate group, these first-generation Philadelphians wanted to see the homeland presented through a more heroic lens. They didn't want to see the Newfoundland of lack, the Newfoundland of want, the Newfoundland they'd left behind when they moved to America to find a better life. They thought we were making fun of Newfoundland and Newfoundlanders, and they wanted to hear about the progress we'd made since joining Confederation. They were severely disappointed. The reception afterward was one of the worst five minutes I've put in in my entire life.

I can tell you about the time Father Jim Hickey—now dead, and a convicted pedophile, but in 1975 still a powerful spiritual leader in the parish of St. John the Baptist—denounced Codco, and all its works and pomps, from the steps of the Basilica. In 1988, Jim Hickey would plead guilty to twenty charges of sexual assault, gross indecency, and indecent assault involving teenage boys, and would die in 1992 while serving his sentence at Dorchester.* Or I could relate what a dreadful time we had playing in a short-lived theatre festival at University College, London. We played for a week and were followed by an American man who danced the Bible. God, I hated England then! It was the summer of 1976, and London was in the midst of a heat

---

* In 2007, I was profiled on the show *Who Do You Think You Are?* and had traced my ancestry back to Enniscorthy, in County Wexford. I was in St. Aiden's Cathedral, and a priest was showing me the baptismal font where he said my great-great-grandfather had been baptized. He then informed me that, as a Redemptorist, he had travelled to St. John's for Lenten Missions. After quite a long and uncomfortable pause, he tentatively asked me if I knew of a priest named Jim Hickey. I said I did, and that he'd died in jail. He looked at me and I couldn't read his expression, but he said, "Oh yes, we thought that might happen to Jim."

wave. The stink and grime of the city stuck to every part of me every time I stepped outside. When we arrived at the theatre (we were late because we'd been trapped in a huge thunderstorm at LaGuardia), there was no one to greet us. The artistic director, who had thrown a typewriter at his assistant the day before and was in the throes of a complete mental collapse, had been sectioned.* In the middle of rehearsal, the stagehands threw large planks of wood at us through the velvet curtains. It was a nightmare. When the run was over, we decided to go for a holiday in Cornwall. We arranged to rent three caravans. When we got there, we were devastated to learn that our romantic notion of gypsy caravans were in fact dirty, dreary old trailers.

That was the year of the Montreal Olympics, and we were invited to be part of the cultural Olympics.** We were picked up at Mirabel Airport by what looked like a full regiment of Canadian soldiers, complete with military battle dress and fully weaponized. I don't think we really did ride into downtown Montreal in a tank, but it certainly felt that way.*** The military escort was a precaution in response to what had happened at the Munich Olympics in 1972.****

Professionally, we were doing great. We were garnering lots of national and international success. Yet it was becoming harder and harder for us to get along, and we were moving inexorably toward our demise.

---

* The word the English use to say that someone has been locked up in "the Mental."
** Greg Malone always used to say, "The cultural Olympics: when you're not acting, you're running in place."
*** Dyan had dropped acid, so the soldiers and the guns and the camouflage completely freaked her out.
**** The Munich Olympics were overshadowed by the Munich Massacre, in which eleven Israeli athletes and coaches and a West German police officer were killed by the Palestinian military organization Black September.

I know that once I got going and found my feet in Codco, I fought my corner with great ferocity. I was fighting desperately to create a place for myself, to be on stage and to get my ideas (as ill-formed as I believed they were at the time) in front of the live audiences. One of the things I found so difficult at the time was pretending that I wasn't fighting. It's difficult enough to compete to get your piece and yourself on the stage. It was definitely shameful for a woman to be openly competitive, particularly with other women. It was perfectly acceptable for there to be open rivalry between Andy Jones, Greg Malone,* Tommy Sexton, and Bob Joy (Bob being the least combative), but we always felt so ashamed that we three women, Cathy, Dyan, and myself, would ever be openly in competition. There was something so socially unacceptable about a woman with ambition at that time, a woman with hopes, dreams, and aspirations beyond getting a fella, getting him down, and getting the baby batter out of him.

I should say here, I know this sounds like the men in the group were particularly misogynistic, but this was not the case at all. All the Codco men were equal-opportunity fighters for the spotlight. And because they were all gay—some in open gay relationships, some more closeted—and society had relentlessly made them feel marginalized for so long, they were much more open and welcoming to other marginalized communities (i.e. women in comedy).**

There was always tension. Greg and Andy had been competing since grade one. Tommy was the baby, and so uber-talented

---

* Andy and Greg had been friends and combatants since grade one at St. Bonaventure's College.

** The question "Why aren't women funny?" is constant and exhausting. Every year or so, a new magazine article pops up repeating it. Will this never end?

it felt like he was getting away with everything. There was tension between Cathy and me, as I already mentioned, and Dyan was quickly losing interest in being on stage at all. And though Greg and I improvised with each other so well, and acted in so many sketches together, we had very little time for each other outside of work. Nothing that he wanted was what I wanted. While Greg wanted to be the director, I wanted there to be no director. Greg wanted his wife, Mary White, to be our manager; I didn't. But although we were often at loggerheads, we managed to write some great comedy material.

At least four members of Codco had totally embraced the Rastafarian lifestyle. They thought that anything outside of subsistence farming was Babylon,* not Irie,** so continuing to work in entertainment meant they were going against their religion. Also, as we each coveted the spotlight, the toll of working collectively had become unsustainable.

Tommy, Dyan, and Cathy bought some land in New Brunswick, but by all reports had a difficult time trying to turn it into a working farm. Bob went off to do a play in Toronto with Eli Wallach and Anne Jackson. The play later moved to Broadway, leading to Bob being named "one of the ten brightest young faces on Broadway." Andy was hatching ideas that would lead to the creation of the movie *The Adventures of Faustus Bidgood*. I was hatching right along with him, but—and I know this is going to come as a surprise—I always felt somewhat left out. So I decided to take off to attend the Instituto San Miguel de Allende in Mexico and study weaving.

---

* In Jamaican slang, this means oppression, chains, and slavery.
** In Jamaican slang, this means not good or great.

After Codco formally broke up and as the '70s progressed, different combinations of us got back together for two other national tours. Greg, Tommy, Cathy, and I wrote a show called *Who Said Anything about Tea?* and toured it across the country. Then Tommy, Cathy, Andy, and I held a series of cabarets upstairs at Bridget's Pub. These morphed into a national tour of a show called *WNOBS*.

In 1979, Andy and I, with a group of dedicated artists and administrators from downtown St. John's, got busy taking over the Resource Centre for the Arts. I worked with Greg and his wife, Mary, on a TV series called *The Root Cellar*, where the Wonderful Grand Band began. In 1981, Cathy Jones and I joined Greg and Tommy as comedians in the band. By 1986, Tommy and Greg were coming off a successful national TV series called the *S&M Comic Book*, and Michael Donovan, an Academy Award–winning producer,* approached us with the idea of us all coming back together to do a Codco sketch comedy TV show. Mary White was Greg and Tommy's manager on *S&M*, and if they were going to be part of Codco again, Mary White was going to have to be the manager. Despite my deep reservations, I remember clearly thinking at the time, "Well, I'm just gonna give up what I think and what I feel, because if Mary is the manager Greg will be happy, and if Greg is happy then I'll be happy." I was dead wrong. It didn't take me long to realize that I only spent about six hours a day at most with Greg, while I was sadly with myself for the whole twenty-four. We produced some great work. We had an extraordinary crew to work with. Bev Shechtman was

---

* For producing *Bowling for Columbine* for Michael Moore.

a makeup genius and Judi Cooper Sealy could turn you into a completely different person just by putting you in the right wig. Juul Haalmeyer was a brilliant costumer.* Michael Donovan had the foresight to hire a lot of the creative staff from SCTV, including John Blanchard, a virtuoso comedic director (I didn't like him that much because he was always telling me what to do, or as others would see it, doing his job). He left us in '89 to direct *The Kids in the Hall* and was replaced by the wonderful David Acumba. All throughout the TV series, we were blessed with the support of brilliant people. The extraordinarily talented CBC Halifax crew welcomed us with open arms and did everything they could to accommodate and support our work.

Doing the TV series was very difficult for me for several reasons, a lot of them my own. It was 1986, I was thirty-four, and my drinking had really picked up. I began to feel worse and worse about myself and therefore started to drink more and more. Clinically, alcohol is categorized as a depressant. I knew this, but I didn't embrace it because every day I thought drinking could lift my spirits and give me a boost through the endless dark night my life had become. But all this time I was just making myself feel worse, crushing my poor little spirit even more, and making the Dark Night of my life as dark as a black

---

* People were always taken aback because Cathy and I were "always big girls for twelve," too big for TV but not really big enough for comedy. Juul never once in the six years that he costumed us for the series had a belt that fit either Cathy or me, and would always say, "Oh dear girls, I'm going to have to use a belt extender." It happened so often we stopped being embarrassed by the size of our waists and began to enjoy the extenders.

cat in a coal mine at midnight.* In the end, I just longed to be unconscious.

In Codco there was always a great furious jostling for power. This was a natural result of us side-stepping the generally accepted patriarchal, hierarchical theatre system that involved a director—an artistic autocrat perched at the top of the pyramid, holding all the power, making all the decisions. There was a lot of tension in the Codco collective as we fought daily for our piece of creative control.

In Codco I never felt fully like myself, or that I had a right to my feelings. I always thought I had to defer to someone else's feelings. This did not begin with Codco, but Codco was no help in ending it. I see now that I had a choice, I wasn't chained up to a table in the rehearsal room. I also understand, finally, that it is my job and only my job to take responsibility for my choices and my feelings. I could have left, but I was afraid to try to go it alone, I had so little belief in my own talent or ability. At the time, I thought the rest of Codco were so much more talented, and I feared I might be nothing without them.

I was so scared of everyone in Codco. Scared to death, really (if I'm honest, I've sort of spent a lifetime being afraid of every living human). But the great fear that I held about Codco was not that they were so scary, it was that I knew I needed them so badly and I wanted so much from them, much more than I could expect anyone to be able to give. Years later, Andy wrote

---

* My sister, Madonna, had five children and was also a heavy drinker. During one of Conception Harbour's worst winters, when she had no money and no wood for heating, she stripped the clapboard off the house and burned it for heat, effectively making the house colder and more unheatable.

a play with a character who was incapable of getting enough love. I saw the show, and when it was over I kind of blithely said to a woman I was working with at the time, "I think that character is me." And she said, "Well yeah, duh!" Her response blew me away. I had no idea that people could see me so clearly. I thought I had hidden all that neediness behind a wall of toughness and drowned it in a sea of hard liquor.

Newfoundland

IT WAS 2007, AND I WAS SO HAPPY I THOUGHT I'D died and gone to heaven. I was working on the short-lived CBC TV series *Hatching, Matching, and Dispatching*, and I loved it so much. It was my first truly happy, looking-forward-to-showing-up-every-day creative experience. *Hatching* told the story of the Furey family of Cat's Cove, who like so many families in small-town Newfoundland, were charged with ferrying their friends and neighbours right from the cradle to the grave. The Fureys owned the ambulance service (Hatching), the wedding hall (Matching), and the funeral parlour (Dispatching).* *HMD* was the opposite of *Seinfeld*, the show about nothing. *Hatching, Matching, and Dispatching* was the show about everything—

---

* While doing our research for the show, we ran into a family from Conception Bay South who ran a dance hall, funeral parlour, and crematorium. The local wags called the business Shake 'Em, Wake 'Em, and Bake 'Em.

life, death, birth, sickness, and even existence beyond the grave.*

The show was like that Nova Scotia brew, Keith's Beer: those who liked it liked it a lot. Some people, however, were outraged by it. They did not find sickness or death to be one bit funny. They found it altogether too, too dark. We Newfoundlanders do have a very dark sense of humour. I come by mine naturally. Let me tell you this story about my oldest sister, Madonna, who, unlike most Newfoundlanders, did not love Newfoundland. People here always say, "You can tell the Newfoundlanders in heaven because they're the ones who are always asking when they can go home."

Madonna did not have the same passion for Newfoundland; the rocks drove her mad, even the trees got right up on her last nerve. She found the big spruces oppressive and dark. She fell in love with urban southern Ontario, and years later when she was dying, she said to her children, "I don't want any fuss, just cremate me and throw my ashes off the overpass on the 401." She loved the 401; it represented freedom to her, I guess. Her children were upset by this and said, "Oh no, Mom, we can't do that," to which Madonna replied, "Fuck ya, then. Do what you want." And that's exactly what they did do. They held a celebration of her life, brought Madonna's ashes back to Newfoundland, and scattered them around the pond in Conception Harbour, the very place she never wanted to be.

On that very same day, I called my sister Laura (a.k.a. Lol)

---

* I approached creating the show in an unconventional way, not as a sketch comedy show or a sitcom, but something that resembled a composite novel (a book of short stories that stand alone, but when read together interrelate and create a larger whole). And that's how I saw *Hatching*: sketches complete in and of themselves that together would contribute to a larger half-hour narrative.

and asked her where she was. She told me she was with Madonna's children and our youngest brother, Greg, scattering Madonna's ashes. "WHAT?" I yelled into the phone. I couldn't believe it. I was gob-smacked, left out yet again. All the time I was growing up, Madonna was my favourite sister. I was always so impressed by her. I remember once when I was about twelve, she said she didn't like blond men because they were too vacuous. I had never heard the word vacuous before and I wasn't sure what it meant, but to my twelve-year-old mind it was an extraordinary word. I found my sister Madonna just as extraordinary.

When Laura got off the phone, my brother Greg asked, "Who was that?" Lol told him it was me, and that I was really mad no one had let me know they were scattering Madonna's ashes that day. "Well," Greg said, "what in the name of Christ is it gonna take? I mean, we gave her away, sure, when she was eight months old, didn't we? And we all went out to Alberta that time and never told her. What are we gonna have to do? Write her a fuckin' book?" I think it was weeks later that Lol told me what Greg had said. When I heard it, I just burst out laughing.

I thought of all my years of secret sadness and pain, all the torment I put myself through wondering why my parents would give me away (I'd never had the courage to ask anybody why they did it. I was so afraid of Mom I could never ask her, and I felt it would seem ungrateful to ask Aunt Mae, Aunt Phine, or Uncle Jack). But now, here it was, the great sadness that had darkened my days, out in the open and being served up as a joke. It was such a relief to me, such a burden lifted off my shoulders. I remember telling this story later in a makeup room to some actors from Toronto and their faces settled into a very sad, almost tragic look. I tried to explain the sense of release and freedom I felt. "It's funny," I said. "Yes," they replied, voices full of pity, looking at me mournfully. "But so very sad, too."

I told this story to a guy my husband and I met in a coffee shop in Rocky Harbour, and we had a great laugh. He matched my story with one of his own. "Once I was the lead guitarist in a band that played up and down the Northern Peninsula," he said. "We were playing in a dance hall in St. Anthony, but there was no one to take the money at the door. Someone suggested we should call Ankles. Ankles, they said, took the money at the door all the time. They gave me Ankles's number. I felt odd calling a stranger by an obvious nickname, the meaning of which I didn't understand, but I called anyway. A woman answered the phone and bawled out, 'Ankles! You're wanted on the phone.' I heard a male voice in the distance answer, 'Yea Mom! I got it!'

"Everything went tickety-boo at the dance. Ankles took the door, and there were no problems. But I was still curious about the origin of his nickname. The next morning, we stopped at a restaurant and asked the waitress if she knew the man who'd taken the door the night before. She said, 'Oh yeah, Ankles.' I said, 'Why is he called Ankles?' A forlorn, though slightly insincere look appeared on her face and she said, 'Well, a few years ago Ankles got right low-minded and tried to hang himself off the chimney. But see, the rope was too long, so he only broke his ankles.'"

I know it's not what you'd immediately call funny, unless,

of course, you are a Newfoundlander; here, it was always expected, even demanded, by my crowd anyway, that you constantly "take the piss," give someone a hard time. This applied especially to family, and anyone else you loved or even liked. If the recipient seemed hurt by your mean remarks, your response would always be "What's wrong with ya, b'y? I'm only given you a hard time." (I always wanted to respond to this with "That is what is wrong with me! You're giving me a hard time!")

But that was the dynamic, the social conditions we grew up in. I honestly believed that the best way to help someone get over a bad situation was to tease or mock them relentlessly until they finally let go and got over it. These days, such an approach seems illogical at best if not downright cruel. Yet even to this day, I sometimes still believe that taking the piss or giving someone a hard time is a merciful, judicious use of mocking and jeering, all in a heroic effort to beat them out of their low-minded and miserable state.

Growing up in Newfoundland, you had to have a sense of humour. It was necessary for your very survival. It was one of the only reasons they'd let you sleep indoors or, for that matter, feed you. I don't know what happened to all the unfunny Newfoundland children. Perhaps they died or something.

When I was young, if there was anything wrong with you, they never took you to the doctor, even if you were really seriously ill with something like bronchitis or tuberculosis. All they'd do back then was put a huge, nuclearly hot mustard plaster on your chest. Oh my God, the searing pain of those mustard plasters. Ha! I'd like to see the tubercular germs that could stand up to the gigajoules of heat in those things. It would practically burn your chest right off. (To this day, I believe that is the reason my breasts are still unnaturally tiny for a woman my age.)*

If you had an infection—in your arm, let's say—they'd put a bread poultice on it, which was nothing but white bread and scalding-hot water. Or say you had an earache. They'd treat that by pouring boiling hot Saint Anne's oil right into your ear canal. All I was missing was a big slice of ham on my head and I'd be a whole human sandwich. You had to learn very quickly to never complain, because as bad as it was, you knew the cure would be so much more painful.

When I was growing up, a lot of babies had Pepsi in their titty bottles. This was as common as dirt. The mothers of the Pepsi-suckled babies would always insist, "I tries to get him to drink a drop of Carnation milk, but no way, he won't drink nothin' but Pepsi, 'cause he loves his Pepsi don't he? Yes he do, yes he do, he do so." And then, said mother would go back to nuzzling and making goo-goo eyes at the Pepsi-guzzling infant. And I can't tell you the endless number of tiny toddlers I saw tied on by a leather harness to a long, long clothesline out in the backyard. All day long you'd see them, plodding hopelessly, endlessly, back and forth, back and forth—little tiny toddlers with a full face load of snot, a tummy full of flat Pepsi, and a psyche drowning in existential dread.

Oh, and the number of apple-cheeked, grey-haired Newfoundland grandmoms who engaged in the daily psychological torture of toddlers? Countless. You'd see the granny with a

---

* One horrible boyfriend wrote "tiny tits" in permanent marker across the inside cup of my best bra. More than sufficient reason to leave him, but sadly I stayed for another couple of years.

baby (her new grandchild) in her arms, looking down at a toddler (her slightly older grandchild) on the floor—let's call the toddler Jonathan—and Granny is saying, "Granny don't need Jonathan no more, oh no she don't, she got a new baby now, oh yes she do." At which point poor three-year-old Jonathan inevitably bursts into tears, to which Gran responds, "Oh don't be such a sooky baby, Jonathan, for Christ's sake, grow up." Then she would go back to showering the new baby with kisses while looking slyly at Jonathan to judge his response. And if he kept grizzling and bawling, she would continue to chide him in the harshest language possible. I've seen this scenario play out so often. We even had a sketch on Codco about it.

So it's no wonder we're dark. And at least half of us, sure, had our knees wore right down to our hip bones from spending so much time on them doing the requisite amount of praying demanded of a Catholic child at that time. Morning, noon, and night. In the morning, as soon as your tender tootsies touched the linoleum, you were down on your knees saying your morning prayers. Then once you got to school, you immediately dropped down on them to recite the prayer demanding God's help to get through that morning. Then to open every class, more prayers, more knee damage, inevitably leading to the Angelus at noon time, then Grace before and after lunch (thank God we didn't need to kneel for that), then back in the classroom for a full slate of knee-torturing prayers to get you through the afternoon.

Not to mention every first Friday of the month, when you were required to attend mass before school, and doing your Easter duty, and crawling around the church on your knees doing the Stations of the Cross. I received the Eucharist on my knees. I made reparations for sins on my knees. Every Saturday it was confession, and of course I confessed on my knees. Every Sunday morning there was High Mass at 10:15, demanding an enormous amount of kneeling. And every Lent, there was the Retreat, for which they brought in a terrifying hellfire-spewing Redemptorist priest from Ireland. Every day for a week, all the Catholic schools around the Basilica of St. John the Baptist would gather to be reminded of the Horrors of Hell and the dire consequences of sin. You spent hours and hours on your knees, for which you were guaranteed a plenary indulgence.*

Then every night after supper, there was at least an hour down on those poor, bashed-up knees saying the family rosary.** Often during that hour, I'd begin to lose all hope. I frequently despaired, thinking I would never live through another rosary. But it always ended just in time for me to get up off my knees, go up over the stairs, and get down on my knees again to say my nighttime prayers and prepare for Aunt Phine to douse me with holy water to protect me against all the unclean thoughts that might invade my seven-year-old mind as I slept. And that's why today knee replacement is the most common surgery (next to open-heart surgery) for Catholic Newfoundlanders of a certain age. We are a people full of broken hearts and worn-out knees. So really, why wouldn't our humour be dark?

I can't say for certain what defines us as Newfoundlanders, but I know we're nothing like the way they portray us in the Broadway musical *Come from Away*—as exceptionally welcoming and generous individuals ready at the drop of a hat to open

---

* A plenary indulgence moves your soul closer to heaven and shortens—actually totally eliminates—the time spent in purgatory.

** Already discussed at length in "The Little Girl Who Grew Up Next Door to Her Family."

our homes, our hearts, and our culture to anyone who happens to show up on our doorstep. We're a lot more complicated than that. Like an old fella from Gander said to me last week about the musical, "Well what in the fuck did they think we were gonna do, Mary? Let them starve to death?"

General Rick Hillier, a Newfoundlander who was once Canada's Chief of Defense staff, would often question whether Newfoundlanders really were that friendly or whether we were just plain nosy. Ray Guy, a brilliant Newfoundland satirist, would always say we Newfoundlanders had a genetic pool the size of a pudding bowl, and that may be the clue to understanding our good-natured friendliness and hospitality. Perhaps it's nothing but a biological drive, just trying to get a leg over anyone from off the island—get them down and, you know, get the genetic baby batter out of them and finally widen that tiny pool.

God alone knows why we decided to stay here on this inhospitable rock and hang on like limpets century after century. Maybe it's because we are an ornery, cantankerous, fiercely independent, generous, funny, and lovely crowd, and we suit one another.

If you were visiting St. John's right now and you were in a taxi coming from the airport, and the sun was shining (good luck with that) and you said, "Lovely day today!" the taxi driver, without missing a beat, would turn around and say, "Oh yeah, no doubt we'll pay for this."

Canada

BACK WHEN I THOUGHT IT WAS BETTER TO PRETEND to know things than to ever let on that I didn't know something, the CBC called and asked me to give the Spry Lecture. I was thrilled. What an honour! Of course, I had no clue what on earth the Spry Lecture was, or what I was supposed to know or do to deliver one. But at that point I felt that not knowing would be highly insulting to this wonderful person, the person who had conferred such a great and glorious honour on me. Having received this honour, to ask what the Spry Lecture was supposed to be or even if it was good to eat would reveal me as the ignorant know-nothing I knew I was, so I simply said yes. Based on the fact that it was the CBC that had asked me, and that Graham Spry had been a Canadian of some note, I surmised, totally incorrectly as it turned out, that they were asking me to give a lecture about Canada, or maybe the history of Canada. Yes, I thought, it must be that.

Now, this was 1993 and I was forty-one years old. Newfoundland had joined Canada forty-four years earlier, but despite all that, I knew next to nothing about the history of Canada. Of course, right away I blamed myself. I had learned at my mother's knee (or rather, at the metal knee joint of my aunt's wooden leg) a great resentment for Canada and all things Canadian. In 1949, during the referendum, nearly 50 percent of the people of Newfoundland, and I wager all the people of St. John's, had voted against confederation with Canada.

St. John's voted overwhelmingly in favour of a return to Responsible Government. We lost the vote, and we went from being a powerless colony of Great Britain to becoming the youngest and poorest province of the Confederation of Canada. From being England's door mat to Canada's laughingstock. I was born in 1952, and during my childhood, anti-confederate feelings ran very high. There was no end to complaining about the shoddiness of Canadian goods and the dour and cheap nature of the Canadian heart.

I didn't even really run into a Canadian until about grade five, when a girl from Toronto named Janet came into our class. She had four other sisters, a father who had a "big job" with the federal government, and a mother who worked. And they had a maid—all pretty heady stuff for my crowd of Newfoundland ten-year-olds. But the truly memorable thing about Janet was the nose cozy her grandmother in Winnipeg had knit and sent to her in order to protect her delicate Toronto nose from the vagaries of the harsh St. John's winter. *Well.* We other grade fives resented the implication immensely. We saw it as a direct slap in the face to Newfoundland, and of course to us. Who did they think they were? Where did they think she was living? As if St. John's was colder than Winterpig! Oh God, we were incensed. And so we gave Janet quite a lot of fairly vicious tormenting over that nose cozy.

For those of you not familiar with the nose cozy: it is a knitted object, roughly the same shape as the nose, with of course two nostril holes and two strings that are attached to the sides of the cozy and tie around the back of the head to keep it snug. Poor Janet.

You know, I don't remember meeting or seeing any other Canadians when I was younger. There were Portuguese, Spaniards, Russians, Poles, all off the ships in the harbour, all of whom we'd see down on Water Street, and the Americans of course, but I don't remember any Canadians. And in school, except for Janet, it was basically just us. (Remember our genetic pool the size of a pudding bowl.)

After Janet, my next important encounter with Canadians didn't go much better. I'd moved to Toronto to attend theatre school and lived in a house full of homesick and lonely Newfoundlanders, all determined to make Canadian friends or die trying. There was a communal houseload of them living right across the street from us, and on these Canadians we set our friendship sights. We made a plan to pay them a surprise visit on Friday night, but being young, nervous, and socially inept, we thought we'd have a few drinks first to make us feel more at ease. We had a lot of drinks, actually, and then we went over to their house and talked at them quite a lot, and then we threw up quite a lot, and then finally they asked us to leave. And the fact that they never tried to contact us again was, to us, proof positive of the essential minginess and coldness of the Canadian nature.

When I began to tour Canada with Codco in the mid-'70s, the country was still feeling very insecure about its identity. I was always confounded, because Canadians all across the country seemed to be so obviously and so recognizably what they were: people who shared many things and held many common beliefs, one of those beliefs being an overwhelming certainty that they were so much better than us "goofy Newfies," as they referred to us in those days. I never fully understood Canada's struggle to forge an identity because we Newfoundlanders always knew who Canadians were: the people who thought they were so much better than us.

So, having committed to doing the Spry Lecture, I came to the desperate conclusion that I would have to do a crash course in Canadian history. I headed over to St. Mary's University and read everything I could get my hands on. I was left with a sense that most Canadians weren't that interested in their history, that Canadian history was thought to be kind of boring, that not that much had happened in Canada really, it was all just Peace, Order, and Good Governance, yawn, yawn, yawn (and that sentiment continues for many people to this day). I don't really know why a country would choose to ignore and not celebrate its own history. I mean, surely the story of seven-year-old John A. Macdonald bravely trying to save his five-year-old brother from being beaten to death with a cane by a drunken babysitter, while not a particularly uplifting story, is undoubtedly as interesting, if not way more so, than George Washington's "I chopped down that cherry tree."

And what about Louis Riel, surely a hero in all the official languages? I mean, isn't Riel worthy of at least as much recognition and celebration as Davy Crockett? And yet I seem to know so much more about Davy Crockett than I do about Riel.

Why had I never before heard of Chief Peguis and his tribe, who saved the lives of the first settlers brought to the Red River area by Lord Selkirk? When the main group of settlers arrived, they found that none of the promised gardens had been planted, none of the houses built. Winter was coming, and Peguis and the members of his Nation brought those settlers to their camp, fed them, and kept them alive over the winter. In the spring they showed them how to hunt buffalo and work the land. Yes, without Peguis and his Nation, there would be no Winnipeg.

As I was preparing for the Spry lecture, I realized that I wasn't the only Canadian ignorant of our history. Where is our heroic origin story? Why have we never made those "myth of conquest" films that allow us to see the stealing of this land as great and inevitable? Unlike the United States, we have never articulated a heroic myth. Where are our Canadian epics, our civil religion of Canadian-ness? Perhaps we thought ignoring all our history, even the good parts, would allow us to ignore our mistakes, poke them away, not focus at all on the past, neither mythologize nor celebrate it, just ignore and dismiss it with the false excuse that it's all too boring. Are we ignoring our history because we are unable to face all of the mistakes we made,* or have we just been too practical, too steadfast, too steady to indulge in all that over-hyped myth-making so common south of the border?** Maybe Canadians simply believe what the German philosopher Hegel said: "All that history has taught us is that we learn nothing from history," and instead we embrace the words of our own great genius, Northrop Frye, who said that we are formed by our geography, we learn everything from our geography, and *where* we are makes us *who*

---

* I.e., calling it "discovering" this country as opposed to "invading" it. As everyone knows, it is almost impossible to discover a place that is already fully occupied.
** At least we have been mercifully spared the horrors of a Canadian *Birth of a Nation*, with all its filthy racism and ugly celebration of white supremacy.

we are. And just look where we are—every inch of this country is awe inspiring. We are rotted out with geography. We're practically choked on oceans; we've got three of them. We've got that big awe-inspiring Arctic, that huge northern mystery, always looming up there behind us. We have 9,984,670 kilometres of good earth, the second-largest land mass in the entire world. And if Northrop Frye is right, and a people's character is formed by their geography, then our character should be enormous, big-hearted, bountiful, and beneficent, because here we are, a people faced with an embarrassment of geographical riches.

We have so much room, so much room to *be*—to be accepting, to be tolerant, to throw open our arms, to be generous. We have room to celebrate all the things we did right, and room and time to try to fix all the mistakes we made, room to be large in our dealings with the world and with one another. According to the renowned thinker John Ralston Saul, everything we celebrate as good about Canada we learned from our initial two-hundred-year peaceful relationship with the Indigenous people*· ** In a startlingly original vision of Canada, John Ralston Saul argues, "Our institutions and common sense as a civilization are more Indigenous than European. All of the best of Canadian egalitarianism has been heavily influenced and shaped by Indigenous ideas."

---

* "Aboriginal People and European Newcomers lived in peace for about 200 years, from about 1660 to the mid-19th century."—The Aboriginal Justice Implementation Commission

** "In the 1500s, Europeans returned to the Eastern shores of North America to establish settlements. In North America, the British and the French quickly became the two dominant powers. These two powers cemented alliances with the First Nations to support their commercial interests."—*First Nations*, Crown-Indigenous Relations and Northern Affairs Canada

As Emily Carr said, "How wonderful it is to feel the grandness of Canada in the raw, not because she is Canada but because she is something sublime that we were lucky enough to be born into, some great rugged power that we are a part of."

The old saying "Familiarity breeds contempt" worked the total opposite way for me and my feelings about Canada and Canadians. The more time I spent in this beautiful, forbidding, glory of a country, the more grateful I was to be part of it.*

---

* Even twenty years later, I was under the false impression that the Spry Lecture was meant to speak to the artistic process and the way the artist had arrived at the product of their discipline. I found out only as I was writing this essay that the lecture was supposed to be about the importance of independent media and public broadcasting. Sheesh! That's a lecture we could do with right now.

22 Minutes

IN SEPTEMBER 1993, I COULD BARELY WALK OR SIT AND spent most of my days lying down wracked in pain. The neurologist I was seeing told me that if I didn't have back surgery I would soon be dragging my left foot. It couldn't have happened at a worse time. The CBC had greenlit six episodes, and we were soon to head into production for the launch of my dream show, *This Hour Has 22 Minutes*. When I was young, I loved the British satirical show *That Was the Week That Was*, which aired on CBC from 1963 to 1964. Each episode was based on the British news of the week, about which I knew next to nothing. But I still loved the show; it was fun and hilariously outrageous. Maybe even at the tender age of twelve I recognized that satire had the potential to be a very powerful and useful tool—but maybe not.* The show had a folk singer, Millicent Martin, who

---

* I was just heading into puberty, so mostly I was mortified at the outrageous changes that were happening to my child body and probably had little time to think about satire one way or the other.

would end every broadcast with a brilliant musical take on the week's events.

After Codco broke up, I worked for years as the program animateur at the LSPU Hall, an artist-run performance space in downtown St. John's. The Hall had a variety of shows at every hour of the day and night, and I thought it would be fun to do a weekly late-night live show at the Hall based on the news of the week in Newfoundland and Labrador. We'd finished the Codco TV series with Michael Donovan and Salter Street Films in Halifax, and it occurred to me that maybe I should think bigger. Maybe the show I imagined happening at the Hall could be national, featuring the Canadian news of the week. I rarely had faith in my own ideas,* but I decided to run this one up the flagpole, which meant talking to Michael Donovan, the producer of the Codco TV series and the president of Salter Street Films.

I was going to Halifax for another job, so I met up with Michael at a little Czechoslovakian restaurant on Grafton Street. I told him my idea, and he was excited by it. Not so much because of the idea of the show, but because Ivan Fecan, the head of CBC programming at that point, was looking to program exactly that kind of show: a satirical take on the news of the week. Somewhat buoyed by Michael's enthusiasm,** I returned home determined to put together a writing and performance team.

---

* But weirdly, I followed through on them to a certain extent.
** Though to say the words "Michael Donovan" and "enthusiasm" in the same sentence could be somewhat misleading. Michael is a man who has mastered the art of no effect.

The first people I approached were Rick Mercer and his partner, Gerald Lunz. At that time, they lived on Freshwater Road, almost directly behind my house on Pennywell Road.* Rick and Gerald had just created an extraordinarily successful, satirical, one-man theatrical show starring Rick. It was called *Show Me the Button: I'll Push It (Or, Charles Lynch Must Die)*. I thought Rick would be perfect for this new show (not that I ever really believed the new show would happen, but just in case). Gerald and Rick were on board, with the proviso that Gerald would be the creative producer. Still not fully believing in the reality of the show, I immediately agreed.

Conveniently, the person I spoke to next, Cathy Jones, lived just down the street, and so I went to talk to my old colleague. Cathy said a firm NO. She said she hated the news, that she couldn't even watch it without falling into a deep depression. "Perfect," I said, "we need that person's voice, your voice, your point of view. You will be the outlier and will add so much to the show." And indeed, I was right. Cathy came on board. Next, I went down over the hill to Gower Street and asked the extraordinary singer/songwriter Ron Hynes if he would be our folk singer and write the lyrics that would encapsulate the news of the week. Ron was in the middle of producing his brilliant solo album *Cryer's Paradise*, and it really broke my heart when he had to say no.

Then I approached Greg Thomey, the funniest man ever. I don't know how we would have gotten through those first

---

* Everything is so conveniently close in St. John's, a blessing and a curse.

few years of *This Hour*, particularly the Wednesday meetings, which Greg dubbed "the Humilitorium," without him. He made us laugh so much that the embarrassment of reading out our half-baked sketch ideas in front of a bunch of po-faced producers* disappeared. God love Thomey, he said yes. And just up the street from Greg was Andy Jones, who was an enormous inspiration for me, so naturally I asked Andy if he would be part of this still-imaginary show. To my great delight, Andy said yes. Sadly, just before we received the final go-ahead from the CBC, he had to withdraw. That huge loss almost cost us the show, but luckily we soldiered on.

The plan was to do a live show in the Halifax CBC studio every Friday night, to be broadcast on the network on Monday. We'd start every week with nothing and have a full *22 Minutes* episode going out across the nation by the following Monday. We had no writing team that first season. Michael Donovan had put together another brilliant team. Henry Sarwer-Foner was our director, with Michael, and Jack Pellham, Geoff D'Eon, and Gerald Lunz as our producing team. My best friend, the wildly talented Patti Parsons, was on costumes. Karen Byers did a fabulous job on our hair, and Kim Ross did makeup for the first couple of years. I can't say enough about Peter Sutherland and the whole production staff at CBC Halifax. The show would have sunk without them. They were brilliant. We'd already worked with them in the Codco series and never failed to be blown away by their extraordinary talent and dedication.

---

* We actually worked with a crowd of talented, fully committed, extraordinary producers. Something I didn't really appreciate at the time because I was still in my rebel-without-a-clue stage.

Many of our early production meetings had to happen in my bedroom at the Cambridge Suites as my back was out and seemed to have no intention of ever going back in. I had two herniated disks and was in constant pain. I was in my first year of sobriety. If I'm honest, I am kind of contrary and cranky by nature, so I can only imagine how much fun it must have been for everyone else to be uncomfortably perched around my bed having those early meetings with me. On top of everything else, I was terrified. The show had been my idea, and it was going to come to fruition and soon. I remember Rick Mercer doing a "We've Got a National TV Show!" tiny dance of joy, and I remember my response (kept to myself, of course)—"Oh dear Jesus, help and save me from having to do this national TV show!" I was shit scared. I was secretly hoping that maybe a nuclear bomb or something would drop and save me from this frightening future. I didn't get the nuclear bomb, but I did get the aforementioned neurologist.

In October of 1993, during the first prep week for the first show, a month after the doctor told me it was either surgery or a dragging left foot, I went under the knife at the QE II Hospital to have major back surgery. I watched the first ever *22 Minutes* from my hospital bed, and it was great. The show was a hit without me. I felt desperate to get back. As soon as I got home from the hospital, at my insistence, we started shooting Marg Delahunty pieces on Bland Street. I was in bed, wearing a red housecoat and tons of gold jewelry. But it would be weeks before I could walk and go in to work. And when I did, I realized that my world had moved on. I had just gotten back on my feet, but on my first day, those feet got knocked out from beneath me. I was immediately informed that I was no longer head writer.

It became painfully obvious to me that there was a general feeling that things had gone so well without me, did I really have to come back at all. To say that I was devastated doesn't go far enough. I was angry. I felt betrayed and bitter, but mostly I felt shame. My old friend shame was back again.

Shame at my body for letting me down at the worst possible moment. Shame at myself for being abandoned all over again,* and this time by my very own show. To add insult to injury, the producers had decided they would be the final arbiters of what did or did not get in the show. Now nothing, absolutely nothing, was the way I wanted it to be. I could have left the show, but that stubborn streak that has always been both a curse and, of course, a wonderful blessing kicked in. I made up my mind: I was going to stay, turn the show around, and turn it back into the show I wanted it to be.

Thanks be to God that I failed in my quest to do that. If Rick, Greg, Cathy, and I had to write, perform, produce, and edit the show, *22 Minutes* would not have lasted. We could never have worked for all those months, seven days a week, twelve and sixteen hours a day. It was a human impossibility. We could have maybe managed one season, but the show would have never made it into its thirty-third. However, for a while there I continued to fight the good fight. But I've got to tell you, it's very hard to lead a revolution against a system with which everyone is happy. The structure that was in place was serving everyone (except me, I thought at the time), and I got almost no support for my revolt. But dear reader, I did not give up.**

---

* See "The Little Girl Who Grew Up Next Door to Her Family."
** Some of my stubbornness would seem, on sober second thought, to be compulsion.

And during those years I was terrifically unhappy. I didn't want to stay under the current circumstances, yet I felt I couldn't leave—it was my show.

Finally, I wore myself out. I began to enjoy the weekly fight for airtime, the Friday night battles for laughs, the Monday night despair when your favourite piece didn't get in. One of the great things about *This Hour Has 22 Minutes*—and it took me a long time to learn this—is because it is so labour intensive and has to move so quickly, it is very, very difficult to wallow in self-pity or keep resentments and recriminations alive. There was just too much to do. It took all the time allotted—first to investigate the news, then to come up with a funny take on the news, then to act out that take, and then to start all over again from scratch for the next week. In those early years, we did this for seven months of the year. Also, because there were only twenty-two minutes in that half hour and there were four of us, we were bound and determined that each of us would share screentime equally (or maybe that was just me). For years, I negotiated our salaries, ensuring we were all paid equally.

Rick Mercer and I were in a weekly competition to get as many funny TV minutes as possible. One great piece that Rick did, that I felt particularly jealous of, concerned Stockwell Day, the head of the Canadian Alliance party at the time. Stockwell had promised that if he was elected, he would introduce a form of direct democracy in which any proposal supported by a petition signed by 3 percent of Canadian voters would have to go to a national referendum. The "interweb" was just becoming madly popular, and Rick had the brilliant idea of proposing that

Stockwell Day would have to change his name to Doris Day, and if 3 percent of the population voted for it on our website, then Stockwell would have to make the name change. We got more than the required number of votes; it was incredible.

Greg Thomey's sense of humour was so different, so endearing, so brilliant. All of his characters (Frank, his hapless and continually lost international news reporter; Lazy the Welfare Bear) were so whacked in the funniest, most delightful way. We always had so much fun doing "That Show Sucks," in which I played this terrible, overbearing mother (in fact my own) named Mrs. Reardon and Thomey played Eddie, inspired by—but in no way resembling—my brilliant brother Frank. Mom (my real mom) would watch TV stretched out on the couch and would kick whoever was unlucky enough to be sitting on the end. Whenever Mom and Frank were watching a Western, she would often be confused as to who was the good guy and who was the bad. Frank would always tell her, "It's the one with the white hat, Mom, I told ya!" to which Mom would reply, "See, Frank's not that stunned."

Thomey and I did "That Show Sucks" in front of a live audience. Mrs. Reardon always gave Eddie a good kicking or took off her slipper and smacked him across the head with it. Sometimes things went wrong. One night, I forgot I had the slipper with the hard sole, and when I whacked Thomey across the head the force of the blow almost gave him a concussion. There were times that I kicked him too hard in the ribs, but other times I went too soft and Thomey would insist, "No, no, no, you gotta kick me harder than that."

Cathy Jones could just do anything—any accent, any character. Cathy was a dream for the writers on the show.* She could lift the script off the page and bring it to life with or without rehearsal, she just had that talent. Cathy and I had done a lot of two-handers in Codco (The Friday Night Girls, Cass and Betty Furlong, etc., etc.). We always worked well together, and I was delighted when we started doing The Misses Es for *22 Minutes*. I think Cathy did Mrs. Enid first, playing the mother of Frank, one of Thomey's characters, and I wormed my way in as Mrs. Eulalia. Then the two of us took the piece outside to Point Pleasant Park or the Public Gardens and became fan favourites as two old bats out for a weekly airing, talking about the news of the day, the latest scandals, the war, or whatever took our fancy that week. I always loved getting outside into the real world and leaving the airless studio behind.

Every Monday morning during the season would find us in the radio room, full of ideas or not, having the first production meeting of the week. I would drop off my son at his alternative school, then beat it over to the radio room for the meeting. As we had no writers that first year, we soldiered on alone. Those first couple of years were very difficult for me. I wanted the title of head writer. I wanted us, the performers, to make the final decisions about what did or didn't make it to the air. I wanted things to be entirely different than they were, but none of that stopped me from throwing myself, heart and soul, into the job of writing and performing in those first few seasons. I started doing Marg Delahunty, but she wasn't a princess warrior

---

* We finally did get writers in year three, I think.

right away. I'd been playing Marg Delahunty since Kim Campbell ran for the Conservative leadership and my character, Marg, decided to run against her. In fact, even before that, in Codco, all the women were Margs and all the men were Gerrys. And so, I played Marg when she still had no last name and when she was was loosely fashioned on Tommy Sexton's Marg at the Mental.

At some point, in 1993 or '94, when I still felt that television was kind of selling out, and a real artist wouldn't be involved in it, I made the decision to at least look like a real artist, and so I cut my bangs straight across the front and started to wear thick, black-rimmed glasses. Thomey asked me if I was making a special effort to look extra ugly; I don't know, maybe I was. I probably thought people would take me more seriously if I looked like Edith Head. I was "never no oil painting," as Mom would say, so I at least wanted to look interesting. I noticed that my new haircut made me resemble Xena the Warrior Princess—well, at least we had the same bangs. I said to Geoff D'Eon, our on-the-road producer at the time, that I wanted to do a sendup of Xena. We were on our way to Ottawa with me as "Housecoat Marg" and Geoff as producer, fixer, and Pretty Well Everything Else, except, of course, for all the things Peter Sutherland did. Peter was cinematography, sound, lighting, camera, etc., etc.

Geoff suggested that maybe Marg could go as Xena Princess Warrior, and that maybe the always amazing Patti Parsons, our miracle-working costume mistress, could whip me up a cheap-and-cheerful version of Xena's costume. So, with a couple of yards of red felt, a ton of gold glitter glue, and the plastic sword that Patti got me from Toys"R"Us ("Housecoat Marg" was already weighted down with gold jewelry and tons of very bad makeup), we were ready to ambush our very first politician. Or was it the awful Conrad (Tubby) Black, once Lord of Cross Harbour but now just another right-wing convicted fraudster?*

People always said to me, "It must have been a lot of fun to do Marg Princess Warrior," to which I'd inevitably sigh and answer, "Oh yes!" But honestly, catching politicians of whatever stripe, in the middle of a scrum, where you got only one chance to say your piece (generally in television, you can do a second or a third take, but not so for Marg) was deeply terrifying. When I was ambushing a politician or celebrity, I had only one chance to say whatever it was I wanted to say, or I felt was important to say, to those politicians and celebrities. And the truth is, I never wanted them to say anything to me because that would only confuse me. So, it was very important for me to just get everything out, and then to disappear before security came to haul us body and bones out of wherever we were—Queen's Park, the West Block, the Legislature in Edmonton, the Legislative Assembly in Victoria, and so on.

Doing a Marg ambush, I always felt shame—my old friend and constant companion. There I'd be in Ottawa, standing in a scrum cheek by jowl with real reporters from CTV, CBC, Rogers, and City. They were all dressed in their Burberry trench coats, with their good leather briefcases, and there I was in fake medieval armour, which was really just scraps of red felt with spirals of gold glitter glue around my breasts, brandishing my plastic sword. Ironically, in the end, it was shame and deep

---

* Conrad Black was convicted in 2007 of fraud and obstruction, with some fraud charges overturned on appeal after a Supreme Court ruling. He still served about three and a half years in prison. In 2019, Donald Trump granted him a full pardon.

humiliation that got me through those ambushes. In the midst of a shame spiral,* it would occur to me that I was already at the bottom, what with my clown makeup and ridiculous costume, and so, "What odds?" I'd think, "Shag it, I might as well go for it." What did I have to lose? Certainly not any modicum of self-respect.

22 Minutes were an equal opportunity ambushers. I ambushed Joe Clark, then Leader of the Opposition; Elsie Wayne, when she was one of only two Tories sitting in the house; all the Reformers; Mike Harris, the premier of Ontario; Ralph Klein,** the premier of Alberta; Prime Minister Jean Chrétien; Minister Lloyd Axworthy; Prince Philip; Sarah Ferguson, when she was still the Duchess of York; Shania Twain; Prime Minister Stephen Harper; Prime Minister Paul Martin—pretty well everyone who had any kind of profile in the '90s. I ambushed Premier Ralph Klein as Marg wearing a cowgirl outfit, with a gun belt containing a pair of cap guns—you know, the little tin guns, the ones you loaded with circles of red paper that made such a satisfying noise when you hit them with a rock. On our way in, Geoff D'Eon casually said, "Don't take out the gun when we get in the Legislature." I barely heard him, but I thought, "Why would I do that?" I spoke to Premier Klein noting that he behaved even worse than some of the greatest villains in literature. I said that even Ebenezer Scrooge, famously villainous, had only said, "Are there no poorhouses, are there no prisons?" He didn't down a load of liquor on

---

* Thomey did an ad for the New McCain's Shame Spirals.
** This was pre-9/11, and all Edmonton security said to us when we came to ambush the premier was "Close the door, we're not heating Edmonton."

Christmas Eve and have his driver take him down to a shelter (poor house) where he could mock and jeer at and generally, drunkenly, abuse the inhabitants.

Whatever reaction Premier Klein had to what I said, and it wasn't a good one, put me off my game. I couldn't remember what I was supposed to say next. We only had this one opportunity, and we'd come all the way out to Edmonton from Halifax. I was in a fix, and I didn't know what to do. Without thinking, I reached for my cap guns and banged off a few caps toward the ceiling of the Alberta Legislature. People were outraged, and rightly so. I should never have done it. You know what, though? It did prove to me, beyond a shadow of a doubt, that it's always very dangerous to keep a gun handy. Because if you've got a gun, and things go wrong, you're bound to use it.

We once set up a sleepover in Ottawa with the right-wing crowd. Elsie Wayne was there, I remember; some cowboy-hat-and-boots-wearing man from the Wild Rose Party in Alberta; and others who I frankly cannot recall. It was after Peter MacKay sold out the Progressive Conservatives and merged them with the Reform Party, something he promised he would never do.* The sleepover was a lot of fun and made for good television, but it also introduced the notion that *22 Minutes* was getting into bed with politicians. And in that sketch, I literally was!

My favourite politician to ambush was Jean Chrétien. He seemed to be so comfortable in his own skin, and he was so funny. I always felt a level of ease when I ambushed him. I felt

---

* Does anyone else remember that the first choice for their party name was the Conservative Reform Alliance Party? The CRAP party.

reassured that, even if I did mess up, we'd still end up taking a great piece back to Halifax with us. Prime Minister Chrétien would save the day no matter what. He could always handle anything. Remember the Shawinigan handshake?*

I got a lot of flack for a piece I did where I kissed Stephen Harper. At the time, Harper was running for the leadership of the new CRAP party and he was anxious to appear open, friendly, and electable. So it was easy to get next to him. (All that changed once he became prime minister and not even real journalists could get close to him or even ask him questions.)** But that day, before he got all the power he wanted, wielding my plastic sword dressed up in my Princess Warrior suit, wearing an extra heavy amount of orange lipstick, I was allowed up on stage with him. I linked arms with him and said I was going to help him become prime minister, that he would never be prime minister if he kept going the way he was going. "You're against everything! You're against Kyoto, and not just the accord, but the whole city, too. You're going to have to start saying 'Yay' to something. If you're ever going to be prime minister you've got to be *for* something. Embrace something. Go ahead, practice on me. Embrace me!" And so he embraced me. And when he hugged me, I kissed him on the lips. Some people say I

---

* Still tense from the night when André Dallaire broke into the prime minister's residence armed with a large hunting knife, intent on killing him, Chrétien grabbed a protester by the back of the neck and chin, forcing him to the ground and pushing his way past him. This was always referred to later as the "Shawinigan handshake."

** Gerri Hall, one of the performers on *22 Minutes* during the 2008 Federal election campaign, asked Prime Minister Stephen Harper a question in her character Single Female Voter. She was restrained by security and later taken away in handcuffs by the RCMP. She did finally get to talk to Harper, who said he had never seen *22 Minutes*, and asked Hall, "Do you like handcuffs?" Creepy.

French-kissed him, but that's nonsense. I did, however, manage to get Marg's orange lipstick all over his face. Whatever you think of Prime Minister Harper, I'll let you in on a little secret: he's a lousy kisser. It was like kissing a stick of wood, honest to Christ.

That kiss caused a lot of controversy, and the right-wing papers went mad. But it wasn't nearly as controversial and hate-producing as the time I ambushed Rob Ford while he was still mayor of Toronto. It was October 2011, and I was only making occasional appearances on *This Hour* at that time and I had to fly home from Harlow, England, where, along with my husband, Don Nichol, I was teaching at Memorial University's satellite campus. On that weekend, I flew to Toronto from Heathrow and met up with the *This Hour* team. I'd been researching Rob Ford, but I had no idea that Mayor Ford was a man who suffered from the disease of addiction. That story had not broken yet. If I had known, I don't think I would have ambushed him. Doing my research, I found some troublesome press pieces, particularly one in *Toronto Life* that talked about the darkness and the feeling of emptiness in his family home in Etobicoke, and this did give me pause, but who would believe that the mayor of the great city of Toronto would be a crack addict?

We waited for Ford on the sidewalk outside his home. I was in my sixties then, and I had on my regular Marg suit. So there I was, an old lady in a felt suit with gold glue, calling out Ford's name. But my appearance seemed to completely discombobulate him. He fled back into the safety of his house, and I stood outside on the public sidewalk, still trying to find a way to make a piece we could put on the air that Monday. Once inside, Mayor Ford dialled 911 and tried to have me arrested. According to the operators, who gave a special interview to the *Toronto Star* the next day, he called them some fairly awful names—e.g., C-U-Next-Tuesdays, and actually asked them, "Do you know who I am? I am the f—king mayor of this f—king city!" The people back at head office in Halifax were terribly worried that I would be arrested because although I'd done nothing illegal, the mayor is in charge of the police and can deploy them at his will.

The next day, there was a lot of outrage. Mr. Ford said that I'd frightened his children, who he said were in his Cadillac Escalade at the time. This wasn't true—there were no children in his Escalade; there were no children whatsoever. It was just me, Marg, in her sad little suit and a big fearful man desperate to hide his addiction and the truth of his life from everyone. He saw me as a threat, though seriously, what I was going to say to him was so mild and so unmenacing—something along the lines of everybody in Toronto loved him and thought the sun, the moon, and the chevron sign shone right out of his back passage. I wasn't even going to make a "crack" about the job he was doing as mayor. Not alarming at all, particularly when compared to the crack-smoking video that the *Star* finally released. Now I am sorry that I made a man who was suffering and living in fear suffer even more. I'd never have done it if I had had some inkling about what he was going through.*

---

* When I got back to Harlow, the news had already travelled there. It was Halloween, and a bunch of students were dressed up as Marg and Mayor Ford.

I LOVED BEING PART OF THE COLLECTIVE OF *22 MINutes*. For years, I alone negotiated our salaries. We were all paid the same amount, but as we became more established and some of us got agents (I did), the whole salary structure changed. We went from "each according to his needs" to "each according to his ability to negotiate."

At some point, Rick Mercer and Gerald Lunz, unbeknownst to the rest of us at *This Hour*, were in negotiations with CBC to do their own show. I don't remember now how we found this out, but I do remember the shock when they left. We were heartbroken. And what a surprise, I felt abandoned.* They took our director, our editor, and our set designer. At first, we felt that their proposed show, *The Rick Mercer Report*, was very much like *This Hour Has 22 Minutes*, and that the only thing it was lacking was the rest of us. We imagined that once *The Rick Mercer Report* began it would be the end of *22 Minutes*. There was a lot of hurt and some anger and heartbreak for a while.

However, we managed to coexist for years quite successfully. The *Mercer Report* was a great show, and I think we all came to understand that Rick and Gerald hadn't been acting *against* us, but *for* themselves.

Though I am loath to reveal this, in truth, I was never very happy on *This Hour*. No matter how well I was doing or how popular the show was, nothing was ever enough. I once got a standing ovation during the live show; I believe it was the first standing ovation anyone got on the show. Instead

---

* See "The Little Girl Who Grew Up Next Door to Her Family."

of feeling elated and grateful and excited, I felt nothing but dread, thinking, "Oh no, now I'm going to have to get a standing ovation every week just to keep up." I lived in fear that I was falling behind. I think I had what Tony's mother was diagnosed with on *The Sopranos*: anhedonia, the inability to feel joy. With anhedonia you get much less pleasure from doing things you would normally enjoy. That certainly seemed to be the case most of my time on *This Hour Has 22 Minutes*, and if I'm honest, most of my life. On *22 Minutes*, there were times of camaraderie and triumph and gratitude, but for me there was also an undercurrent of fear. I was afraid that I wouldn't live up to expectations, that everybody else but me would do well. Sometimes I sat on the desk with the team I'd put together—Rick, and Greg, and Cathy—and felt a deep abiding sadness that they were close and only I was on the outside.*

There's no denying that it was difficult creating a new show every Monday, particularly in the years when we didn't have writers.** But my only regret is that I was not brave enough to enjoy myself. After all, I was surrounded by extraordinary people, a brilliant cast and crew, a successful show, and yet it was never enough. I was never enough.

---

* It's something I still suffer from. I just directed a show called *High Steel*, which I wrote in 1984 with Rick Boland and Ron Hynes. It's the story of my mother's crowd, the high-steel workers, the ones who built New York. I complained to my friend Gill that I felt outside, left out, and she said, "I don't know how much more inside you could be. You wrote the show, you're directing the show, and it's about your family." This made me laugh, but it also made me realize that those powerful feelings of always being on the outside, which were leftover from growing up next door to my family, had never really disappeared.

** During the tainted blood scandal and 9/11, it was almost impossible to find comedy in the news.

By year twelve, I'd had it. I couldn't come up with any new characters, and my old characters had totally run out of things to say. I was exhausted by my need to always do better, write better, be funnier. It was just too much for me, I couldn't do it anymore. Maybe other people with a much steadier psyche could have gone on for longer, but I had to get out.

Taking Hostages

IN RECOVERY GROUPS, PEOPLE SOMETIMES SAY THAT alcoholics don't have relationships, they take hostages. Well, duh! Yeah, we may be drunk, but we're not stupid. We take hostages in order to survive. We need to have someone on hand to look after us, because we are certainly not up to the task ourselves.* Personally, I have a history of chaotic hostage-takings, filled to the brim with destructive drama. I was either up on bust People Pleasing or in a Red Rage of Resentment.

I started drinking when I was about fifteen. I don't remember when I took my first sip of alcohol. It may have started with a bunch of girls, none of whom I remember now, and a bottle of Old Niagara sherry out in front of the VOCM tower on Kenmount Road. As I somewhat dimly recall, I spent most of that night in a blackout, sick as a dog, on the ground throwing up what felt like everything I'd ever ingested from the hour of my

---

* And of course we need someone to blame for everything that is going wrong in our adult, alchy lives.

birth. Or I may have started with my family at Mary Fewers's tavern in Avondale. All the family was there, as I remember it (except Dad, of course, he wasn't allowed to go anywhere).* I remember Mom being mad at my brother Frank because he didn't ask her and her "old dame friends from the States" to dance often enough, and seeing both my sisters passed out, heads on the table, totally blotto. I was so ashamed of them, and that feeling had a bizarre effect on me—it made me start drinking with wild abandon, faster and more ferociously. That's all I remember, because just like with the VOCM drunk, I went into a blackout.** I had to be carried out of the tavern. I think it was my older brother Mike who carried me, which was doubly humiliating since, for some reason or other, I thought that Mike never liked me.

That was in the summer of 1966, Come Home Year, and I was sharing a bed with my cousin Mary*** and any number of other assorted youngsters. I woke up the next morning alone and soaking wet; I'd peed in the bed. I was mortified. I grabbed the sheets off the bed, took them downstairs, and began to shove them into Mom's tiny washer/dryer combo. Mom was in the middle of saying "My, she got some ambition this morning, don't she?" when my cousin Mary sailed down over the stairs saying, in a very thick Brooklyn accent, "Oh, Aunt Mary!**** I tried to

---

* See "Mom."
** Of course there was no end of people ready to tell you what you were at when you were loaded. Later, it occurred to me to say, "If I wanted to know what I was at, why in the f—k would I have spent so much on liquor.
*** See "Come Home Year."
**** Did I mention that everyone in my family is called Mary? It gets very confusing, but stay with me.

crawl into bed with her last night"—she pointed at me—"and I practically floated away. She pissed the bed." And then she laughed, and Mom, fixing me with a look of deepest scorn and contempt, laughed, too. The news went through the house like a rocket, and everyone laughed, all day long they laughed. Now, for a normal person, a person who doesn't suffer from the disease of alcoholism, that would probably be the beginning and end of their drinking career. Blackouts, humiliation, lack of bodily control. But for me, it was just the beginning.

LOTS OF PEOPLE ARE AFRAID OF DYING, BUT FOR MOST of my life, I've been afraid of living. Many people in recovery talk about how alcohol was a portal that allowed them to become the person they always longed to be. Booze didn't do that for me. It just helped me get where I wanted to go: into oblivion. First I felt it was saving me, and then I knew it was killing me. First it quelled my anxiety, and then it supersized it. It's hard to admit, but while I was drinking I lived in total denial and sometimes total ignorance. All the things I had faith in, believed in, and thought were universal laws of behaviour—when I sobered up, I saw them for what they were: sheer lunacy.

When I was only one week off the booze and on a book tour promoting a collection of Codco plays, I found myself in Halifax, miserable, crying constantly. My colleague Cathy Jones suggested that I go see this massage therapist that she liked. I sobbed, "It's not physical, it's mental," and Cathy very wisely opined that "sometimes if you feel a bit better physically, it helps the mental." The therapist, after giving me a massage, said he was also a psychotherapist. I immediately broke down and started wailing to him about my mom giving me away when I was eight months old, and that I had to attend a reception that night, and "How could I possibly get through a reception without a drink?" Without booze, I knew I would be deeply uncomfortable at the reception, and I had no idea what that might cause me to do. The therapist said, simply enough, that if I felt uncomfortable, I could just leave.

"What?!" I thought, because that notion struck me like a lightning bolt. I had never imagined that leaving was a possibility. I honestly didn't know that if you were uncomfortable, you could just up and go. I thought you had to stick it out. Screw your courage to the sticking post. Man up. Even if sticking it out meant that by the end of the evening you could find yourself totally shitfaced, rolling around on the floor, trying to bite people on the ankles (in the nicest possible way, of course). I had applied this belief that I needed to tough it out to all manner of life situations: staying in abusive relationships, putting up with unbearable social situations, working in jobs that filled me with despair, and on and on. The idea that you were allowed to let go of something, anything at all, seemed almost immoral to me.

LIVING IN THE REAL WORLD AS A FUNCTIONING DRUNK is unbelievably taxing. Always trying to avoid any painful truths, working overtime to manipulate every situation just so I wouldn't get in trouble—and yet I always knew that I was in trouble, deep trouble. I never got too close to anybody, for fear that they would see past the phony front I was putting up. As I saw it, I was constantly trying to people please, bending myself into pretzels, but those people I was so desperate to please rarely realized they were required to do the same for me. So I was always mad at someone, resentful because they didn't keep up their side of the contract—a contract they never signed onto or even knew existed.

When I was a little girl, even before I picked up that first drink, I felt outside and alone. I thought I had to be perfect and always above reproach so I could fit in somewhere. But when I hit adolescence, I knew that kind of perfection was totally unachievable for me, so I went the other way. I was exhausted from trying to keep up the act, so I just gave it up. I started standing up against and resisting everything. I became a rebel without a clue. And yet in my heart, I wanted to be part of everything, not against it. I created a phony persona that I thought would be acceptable, first to my birth family, and then to all those other people who I thought I needed to impress. I truly believed, in all my deep ignorance, that my new, tough, hard-drinking, rough-talking persona protected me, and that I could hide behind that front. I believed I had to be what I thought people wanted me to be just to survive. I couldn't show anyone the radically imperfect, poor, abandoned, unloved, and unlovable creature I always saw myself as being. Never once did I doubt that I was a victim.

One of the worst parts of my illness was learning over time that I could never count on myself. Oh, I kept on working, kept on doing shows. I very rarely drank before a live show, and very rarely let alcohol interfere with work.* Yet, always knowing that

---

* That's not really true, because sometimes I would come into work still drunk or so desperately hungover as to be almost paralyzed with anger and resentment.

I wasn't reliable, and that once I had that first drink all bets were off. Living this way was so difficult that I spent years believing in nothing, particularly not in myself. For a good twenty-five years or so I was on an emotional seesaw—I believed I was worthless and had no real value or use, and yet I acted as if I was the most useful, precious, valuable thing on the planet. An egomaniac with an inferiority complex.

I often felt as though I was in a deep, dark hole of some sort, and that the only thing I could reasonably do was to dig down further. No matter how good or bad things were, I could never find satisfaction with my life as it was. Someone else's life always seemed so much better to me. I felt that life had short-changed me, that everyone else was cozily tucked up in their homes, gathered lovingly around the hearth, while I was alone out on some bleak promontory, the wind blowing a gale and the rain and sleet coming at me sideways. For years, my life was just a perfect storm of dissatisfaction, unhappiness, self-pity, and resentment. But, in the face of all that misery, I just kept on drinking. It never even occurred to me that drinking had anything to do with my unhappiness.

My thirties were the worst. On many nights I found myself downtown at three or four in the morning, stumbling from one late-night dive to another, often alone. Many of my former drinking companions had either given up, gotten married, started families, or just died down dead. Even ordering the second or third bottle from the bootlegger didn't hold much promise any more.

When I was thirty-seven my partner Ray and I privately adopted a beautiful and perfect baby. I flew out to Vancouver to meet with Dina, my son Jesse's birth mother, when she was six months pregnant with Jesse. Dina and I had a lot in common, including that she, too, had been brought up by her aunties. We spent a lovely afternoon together in the second-stage women's shelter where Dina and her three children were living at the time. Three months later, Ray and I flew back to Vancouver and took Jesse home to Newfoundland.

Jesse was ten days old when we first held him. We were at the hospital every day, but we could only see him through the glass wall of the infant nursery. Because Jesse was going to be adopted, neither Dina, his birth mother, nor I, his adoptive mother, were allowed to see him or hold him for his first ten days. It was a policy designed to protect both birth mother and adoptive mother, but I think it was really heartbreaking and destructive for Jesse. Imagine coming out of the warmth and safety of your mother's womb into a cold universe where you are alone and unattached, with only highly efficient and busy nurses to care for you. I know the nurses were as kind as they had the time to be, but they couldn't provide the necessary skin-to-skin contact or the hours and hours of holding or breast feeding. To be without all that for ten whole days had to be devastating.

When baby Jesse came in the door, what had once been my house was magically transformed into my home. It was a wonderful feeling: I was part of a family at last. But coupled with that wonderful feeling was a sinking sense of terror. I could never admit this to anyone, but I was desperately afraid. I was most afraid that Jesse wouldn't love me, and then also deeply afraid that I wouldn't be capable of loving him. Having been abandoned as a baby, I knew that I was unloved and unlovable. My initial response was to keep drinking, and to keep on running away.

That's exactly what I did, until one night, on October 31, 1992, after a particularly poisonous drunk, providence intervened and as I sat on the stairs of my house, holding a crying Jesse in my arms and screaming at his justifiably angry father, a thunderbolt hit me. I realized for the first time that though I in no way felt that I was worth the huge amount of effort it would take to get sober, I knew I had to do it to take care of Jesse. Jesse was so clearly worth all of that and much, much more.

I believe I cried more tears when I was stone-cold sober than I ever did during the worst of my drunken crying jags, which were always about the same topic: Mom had given me away when I was eight months old—winge, winge, whine, whine, snot, bawl. I remember the glorious moment when I was sitting up in bed about six months into my sobriety, drinking a pot of tea and feeling suffused with the warmth of knowing that if something went wrong with Jesse (God forbid), I would be there and I would be sober, and I would do my best to fix it. The bizarre truth is that until that very moment I had no consciousness of the huge weight of guilt I had been hauling around on my back for all that time.*

Jesse saved my life.

Even after I sobered up, it was very difficult for me to imagine living life on life's terms. Acceptance was, I thought, a mug's game. I didn't want to accept anything. In fact, I wanted life to straighten the fuck up and start living itself on my terms. I was desperately afraid of my feelings, and I had somehow become convinced that whatever feeling I was feeling was the wrong

---

* Not that there isn't still a dump-truck load of guilt there now. Guilt/mother are almost synonymous, aren't they? But at least when I got sober I managed to shed some of it.

feeling. For the longest time, I could access only two emotions: anger and fear. Looking back, I see that what booze promised me was the same thing as those old ads for the Household Finance Company (HFC). Remember those? They suggested you take all your pesky small loans and roll them into one big convenient loan from HFC. That's how I felt about drinking—that I could take all my troublesome, fear-based problems and roll them into one big Alcoholism Problem. Of course, just like HFC with its usurious interest rates, the payback was killing me and the results were disastrous.

Though I had lived my whole life in a state of fear, I didn't, for years, know how afraid I was. Not until after I began to get sober, and my head started to clear a little, did I realize I was afraid of everything and everyone. If my family of origin had a motto, there would be two of them. One, I think, spoken in response to whatever emotional problem they were facing, would have been "I'm not going to be able to take this," and the other, in response to a physical challenge, would have been "I'm not backing down tonight." Though I never really felt a part of my family, I always wanted to be one of them, so without conscious thought or planning of any sort, I tried to live according to those two maxims.

For years, whenever I got afraid I tried not to back down; instead I exploded in rage. But if the problem didn't back off, I ran away. Sometimes, full of fear, my answer was not to cower in the corner but to fiercely leap forward, teeth and claws bared. My personality was built on generations of alcoholism and all the fear, heartbreak, rancour, and resentment that entails. This has often meant I was as afraid of pleasure as I was of pain. I remember standing, gazing awestruck into the Grand Canyon, when a feeling rose up in me that was so intense I couldn't take it. I had to turn away from that magnificent sight to quell that feeling.

For the past thirty years or so, I've cut music out of my life altogether. It makes me either too giddy or too sobby. I'm either dancing foolishly or crying, again, foolishly. Music confuses me with feelings. Or if I happen to be cuddling my dog and I'm enjoying it, I immediately stop and think, "That's enough of that." I am so deeply afraid I will be overwhelmed in some way and become vulnerable—to what consequence, I don't know. Perhaps it's tied to the same fear I have of walking off the pool deck into the water. I'm terrified of those three or four inches of nothingness. I'm not afraid of the water and I'm not afraid of the pool deck. I'm afraid of that in-between space where you're kind of nowhere. I am, I guess, always afraid of losing whatever tiny bit of control I think I possess.

Like a lot of women, I always sought approval from the outside as a way of building some sense of my own worth, some sense of myself. It didn't even occur to me to start looking inward. Honest to God, I never once took the time to look at what it was I wanted. I never considered that maybe my job was not only to look for someone to want me, but for me to find out and express what I wanted.

I have a sense of rising shame as I look back on all the years I was drowning in liquor and self-pity. But I've got to remember that alcoholism is a disease; it was recognized as such as early as 1956 by the American Medical Association. It's so difficult for people to accept this fact, even people like me who suffer from the disease. We feel there is something fundamentally, morally wrong and lacking in us. It's as if a person who had type 2 diabetes was constantly berating themselves for being a weak-willed failure because they couldn't control their insulin. Like most diseases, addiction/alcoholism is caused by a combination of nature and nurture. I was born with a predilection to be an alcoholic, and then the nature of my nurturing helped nail that in.

Drinking is an obsessive-compulsive disorder. Let's face it, nobody wakes up in the morning with a plan to get so loaded they find themselves coming to on the floor of their home, stuck to the Berber carpet with a combination of their own vomit and blood (that never really happened to me, but it's a story I've heard countless times). It's hard for me to admit that I spent so much of my life sitting on the pity pot, totally blind to the real life that was unfolding all around me, and trying, through the force of my will, to make life the way I wanted it to be, purposely blind to who and what I was and why in the name of God I was like that. But the question of why was only another way to keep myself stuck in the problem. What is is, and couldn't be no is-er.

I've been sober and in recovery for years, and I am just beginning, at long last, to know myself. I am beginning to know my needs, to understand my strengths, and finally, *finally*, to accept my weaknesses. I'm learning to live with all my confusion. From the time I decided to put the cork in the jug, little by little I started becoming part of this world as it really is, not the way I want it to be, and finally stopped running away. Well, I still run away sometimes. Progress, not perfection.

WHEN I FIRST GOT SOBER, I TRIED TO REPLACE ONE ADdiction with another. I got a job with the Grand Theatre in

London, Ontario, to play Josie in Eugene O'Neill's *Moon for the Misbegotten*. This was January after the Halloween I stopped drinking, so I was only three months in and very raw. A lot of my isms were still very active. I felt so alone at the Grand. Everyone else in the company was part of the legitimate theatre: the extraordinary Martha Henry directed; the great Roly Hewgill played my father; and Colm Feore, who at the time was the prince of Stratford, was my love interest. I had to hold Colm in my arms for a whole long Eugene O'Neill third act.

Sometimes during that long rehearsal process, I felt so out of my depth. I also felt, and please bear with me on this, like I had been hired as some sort of side-show, working-class freak, one of the geeks, a creature they'd lock up in a human zoo for the entertainment of the masses. I am proudly part of the lower orders, and I was acting in a play that was severely class-conscious. But I believe now my feelings of side-show freakiness were characteristic of my alcoholic, catastrophizing mindset. They were terrible feelings.*

I was Josie, a simple peasant, a farmer's daughter, who was in love with Colm Feore, who was playing James, an upper-class alcoholic at least a couple of social classes above my character. One day, I was standing at the bank machine, thinking about Josie, and I saw Colm Feore stroll by. He was wearing a long Afghani coat, the hem of which was streeling and strooling in the snow and the muck of a London, Ontario, day. I thought that if my character Josie happened upon James in such a way, she would follow after him just to watch him, to gaze upon

---

* But I got all the best reviews, so sometimes . . .

him lovingly. For some reason, I decided to do just that. As an acting exercise. But then, totally outside of my control, the next thing I knew, there I was, Mary Walsh, completely, compulsively obsessed with Colm Feore (who, in reality, I wasn't really over-the-moon about at all).

It's clear to me now that because I'd only been sober a couple of months, my subconscious was desperately looking for somewhere to put all my addictive behaviour, all my compulsion. I used to blithely say that I fell in love with Colm Feore, but love had very little to do with it; it was all neurosis and obsession. Yet all that compulsion was directed toward getting him in some way, whether he was interested in me or not. During rehearsal, Colm spoke often about his loving relationship with his new wife, and I remember clearly thinking, "Well fuck him, I want him, and I don't care what he wants." Luckily, I didn't get what I wanted. Even I knew at the time what I wanted was just so wrong. But as the accused paedophile Woody Allen says, "The heart wants what it wants."

One of my big worries when I got to London, Ontario, was how I would ever manage to get through opening night without a drink. During my active drinking career, I got myself through the painful rehearsal process and terror of opening night, all in order to get to the big booze-up I was entitled to at the opening night party. I couldn't think how I'd get through anything without booze. Christmas? What about my birthday? And holidays, and all High Holy Days of Obligation?

I can see now that there was no better place for me to end up in early sobriety than on the stage of the Grand Theatre, in a play that dealt so brilliantly with the devastation and misery caused by alcoholism. I was also lucky enough to work with one of the kindest, most talented, most warm-hearted men I ever met—Roly Hewgill, who played my father. Roly had been sober and in recovery for twenty years when I met him. It also was such a privilege to work with the great Martha Henry, and I learned so much from her. Colm Feore was and continues to be a great actor.

In our business, we get very close to people while we're in rehearsal, or while we're on set, but often then it's over and you move on. It was different with Roly. He stayed with me, he came to visit us in Halifax, he always wrote, sent a Christmas gift and a card. I thought it was just me, but after Roly died, there was a massive celebration of his life in Toronto, and people from all over the country spoke about how, after doing a play or a film with him, Roly had become an active part of their life and a good and true friend.

At that celebration, the extraordinary Shirley Douglas reached across the table, took my hand in hers, and said in her perfectly deep, mid-Atlantic voice, "Dahling, Roly has left you to me, I'm to look after you now." And look after me she did. She got me an agent, which I didn't have at that point. And having discovered that I was twelve years in arrears with income tax, she got me an accountant. When a member of my family was accused of a serious crime, I called Shirley, and I can still hear her voice as she told me to "Stay off the phone, Dahling," because Clayton Ruby, one of Canada's top criminal lawyers, was going to call me back in five minutes. Shirley was always there, full of love and advice, and sometimes a sharp correction when needed.

The way all that somehow, magically, worked in my favour was nothing if not miraculous. In recovery, I've realized that the world is full of a thousand tendernesses and that there are always people there to support me, and yes, I guess, love me. I can see now that, for me, putting down the bottle meant picking up a life that was worth living.

Untitled

THE GLOBAL PANDEMIC, OR "THE COVIC," AS A LOT OF Newfoundlanders called it, overwhelmed the world and its economy and left so many people dead and countless families bereft. But strangely, during the pandemic I was as peaceful and contented as I have ever been in my lifetime. Previously, I had been flying around the country like a blue-arse fly. I can honestly say that for the three or four pre-pandemic years my best friends were Air Canada employees, and how fuckin' sad is that? I loved the lockdowns; at last I felt a sense of oneness with the world, we were all trapped in our homes, no one was out there getting ahead of the pack, everything felt equally disastrous, I even darned a sock, just one, and of course, I baked that loaf of sourdough bread. Through the magic of Zoom, I actually spent more time with old friends. We'd get together every Thursday night. I got to pay more attention to who I actually was and I was afforded the time to practice my recovery program with greater focus. For one of the first times in my life, I didn't feel left out. But that's all behind us now, and despite everything I learned back then I knew I'd go back to taking on too much work and trying to accomplish much more than I am capable of doing.

I've started to obsess and frankly agonize, and my anxiety level is up on bust, over the climate crisis. With all of the fires and the flooding and the plagues, things are so bad globally now as to seem almost Biblical. I'm half-afraid to open my eyes these mornings for fear I'll be seeing something else horrifically Scriptural, like the seven-headed beast rising up out of the blood-dimmed tides of the sea, or frogs raining out of the sky, or seeing everyone around covered in boils and pestilence. Oh, I shouldn't get myself worked up like this.*

Is it just me or does it seem like things are going to hell in a handbasket here lately? (Or is that the standard refrain of the old?) I acknowledge I am a bit of an alarmist, but let's face it, who isn't these days? I guess that's why I'm finding horror films so great lately. I used to hate horror films. I lived in terror that I would see an image so horrific it would imprint itself on my eyelids forever and I would be forced to relive that terrifying sight whenever I closed my eyes. I never got over *The Exorcist*. I didn't ever want to see a movie about someone possessed by the devil. Did I mention I went to Catholic school? But I had a crush on some pimply faced fella who wanted to go, so lemur-like I followed him into the theatre and off the terror cliff. My brother was so frightened after he saw it, he had to sleep with Dad for a whole month. And my friend Anne Marie went right from the movie theatre to the emergency room, where it was

---

* My therapist has suggested an SSRI or even a benzodiazepine, but with my history of addiction, I'm holding off until the bitter end. I don't think I need drugs, I think THE WORLD HAS GOT TO CHANGE, said the recovering alcoholic.

discovered that she had pelvic inflammatory disease. But Anne Marie, in her fevered state, and having just watched *The Exorcist*, believed that she had been possessed by the devil.

So you can see why I avoided scary films like the plague. But now, the more frightening the movie is, the more relaxing I find it. It's kind of cozy to watch something play out in front of me that's even more horrifying than my actual, real life, terrifying experiences here on this plague-ridden, burning, flooding, disappearing planet. Oh sure, I think, after I watch something like *The Texas Chainsaw Massacre*, the North Atlantic is lukewarm, all the fish are dead, and the way things are heating up everywhere, these days I'd maybe be more cool tucked into a hot oven than trying to relax in my blistering backyard—but bonus, at least no one's chasing me with a chainsaw trying to turn me into a skin vest. Oh yeah, sometimes a good horror movie reassures us that as bad as things are now, *they can always get a whole lot worse*. Sure, look what's going on down in the States.

And believe you me, the Yanks are not the only ones suffering. As Canadians, we're up on bust, angry and terrified. As Robin Williams said, living in Canada is like living in a really nice apartment over a meth lab. And now, the meth lab crowd want to move upstairs. He also said that living in Canada is like living next door to an insane asylum where the inmates have taken control, and that's certainly what it feels like right now. Oh, the heartlessness and the cruelty of the New American World Order.

Oh, but you've got to love the Selfservatives though, especially their present-day fearless leader, the Boy Blunder himself, little Pierre Poilievre, or little PeePee, as I call him. You know, it's hard to tell with little PeePee; is he just disturbing or is he all-out bonkers? Petite Pete, the convoy coffee boy with the three-million-dollar makeover. Pete prefers to speak in Dr. Seuss–type rhymes:

Axe the Tax.

Spike the Hike.

Which made me think, why just axe the tax?

Why not bikini-wax the tax?

And instead of spiking the hike,

put the hike on a bike or a trike if you like

and send it down the turnpike!

Why does the modern-day right-wing political crowd think that most of the citizenry is developmentally delayed and unable to respond to any messaging more complex than what's found in *The Cat in the Hat* and *Horton Hears a Who!*?

Remember when we used to have socially liberal, fiscally conservative Conservatives? Red Tories, we used to call them, they were thick on the ground, the place was rotted out with them. Whatever happened to all those Red Tories, I wonder. They've disappeared completely, they're gone, gone, disappeared like the "blue balls." The blue balls were very popular one time. Back in the day, when a fella was keeping time with a girl, they were always in agony, down below, according to what they said, anyway. Very, very delicate, the fellas in their nether regions. Always were. Betty White said, "If you want to get tough never mind strapping on a set of balls, what ya need to strap on is a vagina, because those things can really take a pounding!" And hearing this, I often think, "Yes! And while you're at it, why not grow yourself a lovely set of breasts?" If there is one part of the body that only does good, it has to be the breasts. Naughty, yes, but oh-so-nutritious, too . . . a miracle of food production and beauty. Sadly, mine are past all that now, but they're still lovely, like soft pillows. Honest to my God, I'm like a good old-fashioned chesterfield—tough, yes, but still soft and cushiony.

The whole world is shifting to the right, and that's always worked out so well for us, hasn't it? In this country we still talk about discovering Canada. When are we going to speak the truth? That we invaded this country. Because as everyone knows it's impossible to DISCOVER a land mass that is already fully occupied. It'd be like if I decided right now I was going to get on a plane, fly across Brendan's Herring Pool, and *discover* England. Ludicrous, I know. But the English are so obnoxious they could probably do with a good humbling, harsh, genocidal dose of discovering. Oh the English, they are ferocious. They terrorized, brutalized, colonized, and Britified over 90 percent of all the countries in the world. Yes! Over 90 percent. And they certainly didn't do it just on the basis of their dry wit alone, no. Every six days some country in the world is celebrating its independence from Britain. It's the most celebrated holiday in the world.

God, I hate the English, as who doesn't? Or I did hate them, we all did in my highly dysfunctional family. It was one of the few things we could all agree on. Mom had an unreasonable hatred of the English because she claimed they didn't know how to eat. How did she even know this? How many English people did she run into in Conception Harbour? Of course she was right; English food, for so long, was inedible, even for the English. Dad hated the English because the English working man didn't even have a suit of clothes. He used to say, "I've been all around the world—Madagascar, fuck it, Mozambique, fuck it—and wherever you see Mother England or the Holy Roman Catholic and Apostolic Church, you are guaranteed to find poverty, ignorance, and want." (Sometimes he sounded for all the world just like the Ghost of Christmas Present.)

And I was mad at the English because I was so afraid of them; they were so mean to me when I first went over there in 1976. I was young and attending a show at the National Theatre in London, watching a production of *The White Guard* by Mikhail Bulgakov. I was thrilled to be there. It was only my second or third time ever leaving Newfoundland. At that time I always wore about eight silver bracelets either as a tribute to Joni Mitchell or because my friend Patti wore silver bracelets and I wanted to be just like Patti (sometimes I think I wanted *to be* Patti, but more on that later). While watching the play, I moved my arm, and some terribly grand English woman sitting directly in front of me turned around and spat out, "Cease that rattling!" I was paralyzed by her anger. When we were heading out for the interval (it was so delightful at the National Theatre, you could actually order a sandwich when you went in, and it would be waiting for you at the intermission), I was very excited, and I managed to bump into the very same woman. I blurted out, "I'm sorry," and I forget what she hissed at me, but it was something awful (in my experience, snotty Brits are even more snotty when they are attending their National Theatre).

While I was in London that year, I met Ken Campbell, who had achieved notoriety and some celebrity for his nine-hour theatrical adaptation of the science fiction trilogy, *Illuminatus!*.

Andy Jones, who I had been travelling Europe with at the time, had worked with Campbell. Whenever Ken introduced us, he would introduce Andy as the director of the Theatre of Newfoundland, and me as his secretary. And if I dared object Ken would just say in his terribly cutting London voice, the one that practically oozed contempt, "Well, if you're not a secretary, you certainly sound like you are a secretary." I asked him a question once and he looked me straight in the eye and said, "Clever people, always making fun of genius." I'm not sure exactly what he meant by that, but I know it cut me to the quick, and so that I wouldn't burst into tears in front of him, I asked him where the bathroom was, and he said, "Why, are you going to have a bath?" Every interaction with the Brits that year was like that, fraught with condescension. I felt so little and stupid, like a bumbling colonial idiot.

Andy and I stayed with other friends of his: Alan Devlin (whose story Ken had turned into the play *Pilk's Madhouse*) and his girlfriend, Norah. They lived in a squat right in Whitechapel, the haunt of Jack the Ripper. Alan later became quite famous, he even made it into the pages of People magazine, because when he was playing Sir Joseph Porter in the Gaiety Theatre's 1987 production of *HMS Pinafore*, apparently drunk to the wide world, he turned to the audience and said, "Fuck this for a game of soldiers, I'm going home!" He strode off the stage, clamoured through the orchestra pit shouting, "Finish it yourself!" and vanished. Still dressed in the costume of an admiral, Devlin went across the street into Neary's bar. They say he drew his sword and demanded a pint. He was terrifying, you never knew what he would do next, and so were they all, all the English.

But now I am totally conflicted and confused about them. I recently had this wonderful trip to London. I stayed in a gorgeous hotel on the Strand. I was taking part in an ITV show called *DNA Journey*. Through DNA, it was discovered that I am related to the famous British comedian Julian Clary, and ITV flew me over to London to meet with him and be on an episode with him and Jo Brand. I thought it was because, although we were only distantly related, we'd both gotten in trouble for saying outrageous things to politicians. Julian had me beat by a country mile. In December of 1993 he made an infamous appearance on the British Comedy Awards. He came on stage and made a joke that compared the set to Hampstead Heath (some of which is known as a cruising area for gay men) and said that he had just been backstage fisting Norman Lamont, Chancellor of the Exchequer. Lamont was in the audience and had presented an award earlier in the ceremony. The audience laughed uproariously, and Lamont himself didn't complain, but the *Daily Mail* and the *Sun* launched a campaign to have Julian banned from television. Despite all that, Julian prevailed. My ambush of Rob Ford had nothing on that.* Julian was wonderful. I spent a great day at the Palladium (where Julian was starring in a Christmas pantomime) and had the best time with Julian and Jo Brand and the whole ITV crew.

And on that trip, everyone in London was kind, almost pleasant. People chatted to me on the Tube, they exchanged opinions with me while we stood in line for the theatre, waiters were not that rude in restaurants. I couldn't figure it out. Why were the English so different to me than they'd ever been

---

* See "22 Minutes."

before? But then, the answer struck me: the English are famous for loving and caring for old things. And now there I was, an Old Thing!*

Remember when Britain and America were in a kind of contest to see who could fuck themselves up the most? For a minute, it seemed like the Brits were definitely in the lead, what with Brexit and fourteen years of continual Conservative government. Yes, it definitely seemed like they were winning there for a while, but they forgot that America still has that Trump card.

IN AMERICA, IN ORDER TO PROTECT THE KIDS,** MANY states have already armed the teachers. I thought, "Gentle German Jesus!" They must have gone to a different school than I attended, schools that were not run by Mercy Nuns or Irish Christian Brothers. My anxiety flies up on bust when I start to imagine what my life would have been like back then if the Nuns had Glocks or Berettas! Oh the terror, Nuns Armed to the Teeth! Nuns with Guns! What a nightmare scenario that would have been.***

I went to an all-girls Catholic high school called Holy Heart of Mary Regional High School for Girls (we called it Hearty Hole of Mary Regional High School for Girls, as who wouldn't?). Holy Heart appeared to be devoted entirely

---

* Of course, the obvious answer was that I'd changed, and I felt a lot less intimidated by them and a lot more comfortable with myself.

** The more Americans insist that whatever draconian measures they are putting in place are there to protect the kids, the more I begin to deeply worry about the well-being of kids everywhere.

*** I went to the Nuns for thirteen long years. Of course there are almost none of the Nuns now—Nuns are nearing extinction. Evolution, which has been so hard on the dodo bird, was inexplicably kind to the Nuns for so long.

to the repression, oppression, and suppression (all the pressions probably) of Catholic girls. The principal, Sister Mary Nano, was in my memory at least 10 feet tall and just as wide across. She roamed the hallways, always on the lookout for evil girls whose regulation uniforms would not reach the floor when she forced us to our knees. Once, Sister Mary Nano, after she'd given me a good smart smack up the side of the head, remarked that I was a bold and saucy girl, I would never get anywhere, and I'd be lucky to get a job slinging hash in a Chinese restaurant. Thankfully, the phrase "Discretion being the better part of valour" kicked in, and I refrained from remarking to Nano, "Most Chinese restaurants, Sister, simply didn't sling hash, as far as I know." God alone knows she would have probably blinded, crippled, and crucified me if I'd piped up with that.

One of the scariest nuns I ever had was Sister Margaret Mary Alacoque. God help us, we all would've been dead if Alacoque had been packing. She was our grade ten homeroom teacher, and she was violently out of control. If she wasn't banging your head on your desk, she was hauling you out of it by your hair. In those days, nuns chose their nun names based on the saints to whom they had the greatest devotion. I'm assuming that Alacoque had a devotion to the famous Saint Margaret Mary Alacoque, who was made a saint because back in the seventeenth century or sometime, she took care of sick soldiers. But not *any* sick soldiers, just the ones who were suffering from the most odious, ulcerated, running sores. They say that every day, the saint would lean in and kiss those stinking, leaking sores. I don't know if she French-kissed them, it didn't say anything about that in *The Lives of the Saints*. But that wasn't enough "mortification of the flesh" for Saint Mary Alacoque. She also made a commitment to only drink water in which those soldiers' filthy, pus-y socks had been washed. God, so many holy books are hard to read, aren't they? Like the Bible. There's so much blood being spilled in the Bible all the time, you start to get this coppery blood taste in your mouth. I read the children's book of the Old Testament to my son and I had to stop. The violence was off the charts, right up there with Grand Theft Auto. And *The Lives of the Saints*, now there's a book that should be banned, it's just torture porn, page after page after page of violence and trauma. But for those who devoured the Fifty Shades of Grey series, wait till you read *The Lives of the Saints*, you're gonna love it.

So many people still insist that this is a very dark and unholy time. As proof, they point to the fact that there are very few new saints being canonized these days. They neglect to notice that if you were getting up to the kind of stuff Saint Margaret Mary Alacoque and her saintly crowd were getting up to nowadays, you'd just have an app on your phone, or your own website, www.suckingonfesteringsores.com, devoted entirely to that nauseating practice. Or at least have your own episode of *My Strange Addiction*.

I ALWAYS WANTED TO BE A WRITER, A NOVELIST REALLY.*
I wanted to write stories. You see, books saved my life, they

---

* As soon as I gave up wanting to be a nun. I gave that up at about age five and a half, after I'd spent six months in the company of Sister Maria Borgia, our ancient kindergarten teacher. Yes, those Borgias. The great poisoners and murderers and saints, too, I can only presume.

gave me a whole world to get lost in. I spent a lot of time alone when I was young. People always ask me what book influenced me the most when I was growing up. (Well, if I'm honest, nobody ever really asked me what book influenced me the most, but I've been dying for someone to ask me.) The book I feel had the most profound influence on me was *Pookie in Search of a Home* by Ivy Wallace.

Pookie was a flying rabbit who lived with Belinda, the woodcutter's daughter. In the book, the inhabitants of Bluebell Wood resort to civil disobedience to defeat developers who are set on felling the creatures' homes to make way for a road. With Pookie leading the charge, the woodland folk sabotage all the work by night and hide all the workmen's tools in the nearby Gloomy Wood, thereby bringing the planned destruction to an end. The story is all about the power of community, and by extension, about collective action.

Matthew Parris, a political commentator in the right-wing *Spectator* newspaper in Australia, has said that Pookie made him a Tory. I don't for the life of me see how Pookie the Flying Rabbit could possibly have made anyone a Tory. Parris talks about the third book in the series, *Pookie Puts the World Right*, in which our hero tries but fails to get rid of winter. Parris wrote that in the book the rabbit realizes, and I'm quoting Parris here, "that lazy or foolish animals with ill-sited burrows or nests have to be shown their folly and every creature given an incentive to work hard, prepare, and store." Now, how Mr. Parris could have gotten that out of *Pookie Puts the World Right* is beyond me, but you know the right-wingers, they can twist and turn anything to suit their own plans for total world domination.

Pookie made me a collective creator, and at a time when the

climate and the seasons are irrevocably changing and humans with ill-sited burrows are being regularly flooded or burned out, Wallace's stories now mean even more to me. They stand these days as eco fables.

When I was eight, my cousin Mary and I set out to write a novel. We named the book *May Woodberry and Her Adventures at School*. Of course, May is a derivative of Mary (we didn't want to stray too far from the family name). We started that book, but we never finished. Big deal, right? For some people, what happens to them when they're little, or how they triumph or fail when they are children, stays with them for their whole lives. That was me. And I thought, this is who I am, someone who starts things and never finishes them. I went on for years believing that. But then suddenly, there I was, sixty years old, and I realized that what I really was was someone who always desperately wanted to do something (write a novel), but who tragically dropped dead before they got up the guts to do it. That thought woke me up. So I wrote a novel. It was called *Crying for the Moon*. It was a coming-of-age mystery and a Canadian bestseller, and I was so, so happy when it got published, I was over the moon, I thought I don't care if no one ever reads it, I don't care if it never wins any prizes, I am just delighted that I finally wrote it. I was so happy I thought I was never ever going to be unhappy ever again. But then, inevitably, someone pointed out to me that everybody has one book in them, and if you're going to be a real writer, you've got to write at least four or five. Jesus, I thought, it took me over sixty years just to start the first one; here's hoping I can get the next four banged off a lot quicker than that.

Change

CAN ANYONE EVEN REMEMBER THE ME TOO MOVEMENT anymore, and how world-changing it promised to be? It seems so long ago now, doesn't it? Remember how we all came together then, and fell back as one, in alarm, shocked and appalled at learning that Harvey Weinstein had forced young women to watch him jerk off in potted plants, a repulsive picture to say the least. And one that, once it lodged in my brain, was almost impossible to rip out again.* We all swore we would never go back there again, that we would finally stand up for our rights as full-fledged, equal human beings and defend to the death women's right to say NO. To at last be in charge of our own bodies. And we honestly believed back then, that if we hadn't entirely managed to knock the patriarchy down, well, we were at least beginning to stagger it. It felt so liberating, especially for the women of my generation.

---

* But old Harvey was just the tip of the repulsive male iceberg. Epstein, Prince Andrew, Jian Ghomeshi, Bill Cosby, Peter Nygård, there are so many of them that at my age I can't afford to devote any more time to naming these miscreants, you know who they are anyway.

You see, my crowd never truly believed that our bodies belonged to us. We were raised to believe, as daughters, mothers, wives, that our bodies were always and forever in service to someone else, to some greater cause. And so, we never thought we had the right to demand bodily autonomy, let alone say "no" to anyone. Back when I was a girl, saying NO to a fella, under whatever circumstances, was never viewed as a viable option.* In my day, if you happened to find yourself alone with a fella out on a "date," you spent the better part of the night defending the territory of your own body against what seemed to be a determined, dogged, invading marauder. Being very careful all the time, of course, not to give any offense to that marauder for fears that some of that terrifying, testosterone driven, male energy would be violently unleashed upon you. Besides, back then the common wisdom was that every girl needed a fella. If you didn't have one, God alone knows what would become of you. You could find yourself in the unenviable position, of being scorned and reviled, and cast out as a sixteen-year-old SPINSTER. I misspent a lot of my youth in the back seat of some shitbox, parked down to the sand pits, in the arms of some gormless galoot. Once there, I found myself trapped, in what seemed, at the time, to be a sort of sexual Siege of Leningrad, forced to spend most of the night fighting off his Russian fingers, trying to control his *Roman hands*. Usually by the end of those nights, I'd be so rattled and worn down, I'd start believing that maybe my body really didn't belong to me at all, but by rights it belonged to the marauder who paid for my Coke out at the Pink Poodle and

---

* Goddamn Molly Bloom and her endless litany of yeses. All those relentless yeses. Written by a man, of course.

was therefore entitled to grab at me with all the single-minded focus of a cheetah chasing down a wounded gazelle. Sometimes in the middle of it I'd feel so flustered, so discombobulated, I'd be tempted to do something loony like lift my leg and pee on myself. Just to mark myself off as my own territory.

So you can imagine how my spirits rose, how hopeful I became, during those salad Me Too days, believing that finally, we women would achieve gender equity. I watched with glee as the younger generation of women held men's feet to the fire as the Me Too movement took shape.

But boy, have things changed! Like most of my generation, I had been labouring under the false assumption that we were in the process of straightening things out, at last. We were moving society forward, and we had evolved so far, it would be impossible to ever push us back again. How could I have been so naïve? But ever since the grab 'em by the pussy, former friend of Jeffrey Epstein, proud women's rights destroyer, Trumpelthinskin has come to power, he has unleashed misogyny akin only to that found in *The Handmaid's Tale*. The Trump presidency and the global shift to the right has threatened decades of women's progress, pushing us back toward the barefoot-and-pregnant-in-the-kitchen stereotype. Incel culture has weaponized hatred against women, the huge increase in domestic violence is staggering, and relentless sexist and abusive attacks on women has grown in number and in severity and has surged across social media.*

* * *

---

* Right now in 2026, whatever gains we'd made with civil rights, with racial and gender equity, are being rolled back at a shocking and dizzying pace.

LIKE MOST WOMEN I HAVE HAD TO BE, SINCE BIRTH, steeped and stooped and ceaselessly trained in the ways of men. I've had to learn what men think, what men like, what men want. And I've worked hard to learn all that stuff, and to use that knowledge to keep myself relatively safe.* Through time immemorial, the powerless have always needed to know the workings of the powerful in order to survive.

Think about all of the thousands upon hundreds of thousands of glossy magazine pages that have been, and surprisingly still continue to be, devoted to the getting and the keeping of a man and the proper way to care for, feed, and pleasure one in captivity. Surprisingly, precious little has ever been written about how to get rid of one once he has ensconced himself in the home environment. The present-day domestic male, they're like ticks really, once they burrow their way in, short of calling in Ace Pest Control, you've got a devil of a time trying to dislodge one.

Has anybody but me noticed how much time the fellas are spending over at the gym? Constantly gulping down steroids, lifting weights, bulking up even further, trying to take up more space on the planet, while we women are over here chained to a Stairmaster, living on Diet Coke and the odd Kleenex tissue, for roughage, desperately trying to disappear off the face of the earth.** That, and always being available to provide blow

---

* As long as I'm not out alone at night, or getting drunk, or wearing short skirts, or displaying plunging necklines, or giving the wrong signals, or not saying "no" loud enough, or . . . well, you get it.

** Why? Why would women want to get smaller? Weaker? Less powerful? I don't know, could it be to avoid appearing threatening to those steroid-fuelled men over at the gym, and thus, inadvertently getting up on their last nerve by boldly taking up too much space, or even accidentally being too loud, or, heaven forefend, being mouthy?

jobs, and never wearing any underpants, and keeping ourselves totally hair-free from eyebrow to toenail. That is what they were trying to pass off as third-wave feminism. Oh, Christ on a Crutch! And of course we are still celebrating something we like to call International Women's Day. For God's sake even root vegetables get a whole week, oh yes, International Turnip Week is October 7–14. And the month of May is International Pecan Month. A whole month for nuts! And women still only get a day? International Women's Day—it's like International Groundhog Day. On that one day, the International Woman is permitted to crawl up out of the darkness, and, if the International Male doesn't brain or otherwise assault her, she can, at the end of that day, scurry back down into her seemingly Bottomless Pit of Inequality, where she can continue to do 66 percent of the world's work and get paid a lousy 71 cents for every buck a man makes. Continuing to do the $12.5 billion of unpaid care work women do EVERY DAY. Thus predicting that the dark winter of Gender Inequity will go on for another year.

As a young woman, I never felt comfortable in my own skin and felt I had to lie about everything, even who I was, because I was so deeply fearful of the world and of course, terrified of men. Told by all the older women in my life that all men wanted the one thing,[*] I knew what I wanted (or at least what I was told to want). I wanted them to want me, and I was ready, and society told me I should be ready, to do whatever it took to get them to want me, because that was my job, to be the object of some fella's desire. Secretly, though, I felt a certain contempt that men

---

[*] I can't tell you how many times I've heard, "Why buy the cow when you can get the milk for free?"

were nothing but a bunch of skin hounds. Hounds of course are a particular kind of dog. And we do call men dogs, don't we? Or currs, mutts, mongrels. In my experience there is some truth to that because men are like dogs in some ways, aren't they? The smaller ones of them *do* tend to be more nervous and aggressive, and men and dogs both share an inordinate fascination with women's crotches. But where they are profoundly different is that even the stupidest dog understands what NO means.

Though we felt we'd made huge, enormous progress on women's rights, there is now a powerful pushback. Women and their sexual and reproductive rights are under threat from all sides. Men still continue to be cushioned by the intact system of male privilege. The privilege that includes the fact that 53 percent of the world's population continues to know everything there is to know about the other 47 percent. What in the name of God can we women do? Personally, I've chosen a small act of rebellion. I'm taking a page from the Broverse, the Manosphere. Those Dudes outright refuse to go see anything they've labelled "chick flicks," they wouldn't be caught dead reading "chick-lit," as if 53 percent of the cee-esing, em-efing population in this world is not worth knowing anything about and doesn't have a decent story to tell. I've set an intention for myself that for the rest of this decade, there will be no more dick-flicks for me, no more dick-lit* either, or maybe even no more dick generally, I don't know, we'll decide on that later (it'll depend on the dick I guess, and what's attached to it). But for right now I am boycot-

---

* God help my generation. We felt it was our duty to read all the "Greats" of the American Library of Misogyny. Norman Mailer, John Updike, Philip Roth, Saul Bellow, etc., etc. As a young woman, tragically I thought myself as deeply disgusting and repulsive as those writers found all the women they wrote about.

ting those weapons wielding, death toting, up on bust, nuclear nihilist, Dick Movies. The ones that always have at least a side story that includes the killing, maiming, torture, and degradation of a woman, or a lot of women if it's a real blockbuster.

Change may feel like it has stalled, even reversed, but resistance remains possible. If the world insists on pushing women back into the shadows, then every act of refusal, every "no," every boycott, every assertion of our own voices and bodies, matters. The fight isn't over—not by a long shot.

Brassy Bit of Aging Crumpet

To me it seems that youth is like spring, an overpraised season. More remarkable for biting east winds than genial breezes. Autumn is the mellower season, and what we lose in flowers, we more than gain in fruits.
—Samuel Butler

I AM HAPPIER NOW THAN I HAVE EVER BEEN, AND IT'S not because I've fundamentally changed, or been born again into the arms of our Lord and Redeemer, or turned into one of those happy clappy people—in fact, I feel it has almost nothing to do with me at all; I'm just happier. All I can figure, the only real change I can see, other than getting sober, is that I have somehow or other, through the process of aging, managed to become a whole lot more like myself and finally figured out who myself is. And honest to God, that is so relaxing, because of course—and it's so obvious to me now, but I swear I was totally blind to it before—it is me, myself, who I'm with all the time. If you're going to spend 24/7, 365 days of the year in somebody's company, it's good to know them a little and not have to live in desperate fear all the time, afraid to get to know them or even look at them very deeply in case any minute you might discover something unspeakably evil or broken about them.

Look, I am so grateful to have gotten this old, to have been given the opportunity to know who I am, in all my petty, mean-minded, open-hearted, self-hating, self-destructive but still pretty good for all that, self. I have to say, it was a relief to finally lay down the burden of that "weird other, much better, kinder, more generous, whole lot funnier than me" person I was always pretending I was. The one I was sure that other people wanted me to be. Yes, that all-round superior person, who was kinder and better in every way.

I've since discovered, to my shame, that a lot of my past kind acts were really more along the lines of contractual acts than actual "acts of kindness." "Oh yes," I'd say in my heart, "I will perform this kind act for you, but my expectations of what you'll do to repay me are already way, way, way off the chart." The other person was blissfully unaware that they'd gotten into a contractual agreement with me, and so they mostly failed to keep up their end of my imaginary bargain, leaving me feeling martyred, rancorous, and resentful, and having to work even harder to pretend to be that fictitious good, better, kind, giving, bullshit person I thought I had to be. It took so much energy* to try and twist and shape myself into some imaginary Mary

---

* And gallons and gallons of hard liquor. See "Taking Hostages."

Walsh, who would be more acceptable to the world at large (and of course, to Mom).*

Nobody cared (least of all Mom), but I didn't realize that at the time. I didn't know the world wasn't paying that much attention to me. This is something I find deeply comforting these days, but when I was young, it terrified me. I thought that without attention I would wither and die. I spent decades fruitlessly looking for the needle of myself in the haystack of someone else's eyes. Which of course is a foolproof formula for deep unhappiness.

I feel very different about things now. My new shorter future suits me to a T and has proven to be much less frightening. It's almost as if the shorter my future becomes, the happier I become, and the more I am able to enjoy each and every day. A limited future somehow or other suits me so much more.** When I was young, I felt so strongly that I didn't belong, I spent most days deeply fearful and unhappy, imagining a long, dark, miserable, seemingly limitless future stretching out in front of me in a relentless and ceaseless way. Now in my seventies, when I'm no longer faced with a series of nerve-racking possibilities, and when I already know what's lurking around the corner, I'm not as fearful anymore.

---

* For more on Mom, see "Mom."

** I'm like the Newfoundland cod fishery. It was said that at one time the Grand Banks were teeming with cod fish, to the point where in 1497, John Cabot and them just dipped their baskets into the ocean and hauled them up full of cod. Cod was everything to us and so plentiful, so present, we treated it like nothing. Men would offload their catch using pitchforks. People ate so much cod they became sick to death of it. We could see no end to the bounty, and so we cared nothing for it. Since the moratorium that took place after the cod stocks almost disappeared, we now treat a feed of fresh cod like it was the nectar of the gods and savour each mouthful of this scarce and delicious delicacy.

I think the secret to my happiness is just hanging on long enough to get used to myself and to the world. Neil deGrasse Tyson tells us we are made up of the same elements as the universe; we are not only in the universe, the universe is in us. And learning this, my fear of not belonging, of never being part of, really became moot. I'm part of everything, part of the whole shebang, and everything is part of me.

Oh yes, my life really started picking up around fifty, and thanks be to God it did pick up, because you know that's the time when everything else started falling down. The legs, God love them, are the last to go. But every year the rest of me dips, drops, and plunges just a little farther down. My eyelids, my cheeks, my neck, my knees, my arches, even my toes. Oh yes, they'd take a dive, too, if they thought they had anywhere to go, the bastards.

What said missus my neck, my back, my duckie, and my crack. But you know what I'd say? What odds. These days I'm like Eva Tanguay—I don't give a dang-way, 'CAUSE I DON'T CARE.

When I turned sixty, that's when things started to seem really good. They weren't, of course. I mean, if anything, things on the outside got worse. I was diagnosed with emphysema,* so I felt myself teetering on the edge of certain death every time there was a draft or I got a sniffle. And yet despite that, I experienced all kinds of happiness. Someone I loved went even deeper into the hell of addiction, and yet I managed through the pain to eke out some joy and light for at least a part of every day. Oh yeah, nothing was easy, and yet there I was, happier than I'd ever been.

Now, for a long time I thought that only I was feeling that

---

* Misdiagnosed.

way, but I've discovered what I'm feeling is common, common as dirt, common as sunshine. No one talks about it very much, but science has now pretty well proven that everyone gets happier as they get older.*

And isn't it amazing? In fact, life is not what our youth-obsessed culture insists it is. It is not a long, slow decline into a sad and gloomy old age that leads inexorably into the grim valley of death. In fact, what many longitudinal and large-scale studies have shown is that when you scientifically measure life's happiness and plot it out on a graph, it will actually show a U-bend toward a much happier old age. I was so surprised to learn that according to multiple studies, old people are the happiest people. And that is despite the condition of our health, or how many bucks we have in the bank. Of course, wouldn't you know it? Men tend to be happier than women. Though women smile more.

Oh, my aching jaws.

WHEN I WAS YOUNG, BACK BEFORE THE EARTH HARD-ened, during those horrible, heartbreaking, and difficult adoles-

---

* The Happiness Curve, as seen here, was first extensively examined in a 2010 study called "A snapshot of the age distribution of psychological well-being in the United States" published in *PNAS* by lead author Arthur Stone.

THE HAPPINESS CURVE

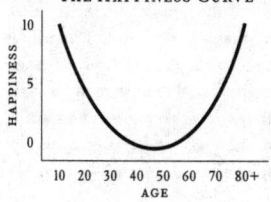

cent years—you remember them, don't you? When everyone was mad at you all the time, and your hormones were always up on bust, and you were spinning around like a mad thing, knocking over things, and crashing into priceless objects. Those years when you had no idea where you ended and the world began, and your breasts were just starting to pop out. Oh, the deep shame you felt to have two big globs of fat stuck out on the front of you, bold as brass. Even today, I'm still suffering chronic back problems from my constant attempts to close in my poor young adolescent body trying to hide those budding breasts. Of course, that proved to be a totally fruitless effort. Those were the same days when adults were always saying to me, "Enjoy yourself now, Mary my dear, because this is the best time of your whole life." And I used to think, "Oh Gentle German Jesus, if this is the best time of my life I'm just going to have to go hang myself somewhere."

Thanks be to God, it turned out the adults were completely wrong about that.* I am happier now than I have ever been, and here I am a brassy bit of aging crumpet on the very slippery slopeside of sixty-nine and really starting to pick up speed. I'm trying to remember what that columnist in the *Toronto Star* called me. Oh yes, a "big, loud, opinionated old bag," and I know he meant that in the nicest possible way. And in *so* many

---

* Another thing they were completely wrong about: In those days, adults seemed totally convinced that no one would ever buy the cow if they could get the milk for free. Well, these days, lots of people are still buying the cow, or getting married, as it is more commonly called, even though, according to what you can hear, fellas are getting gallons and gallons of free milk. That statement is wrong in so many ways, I can't even begin to list them. And what about the Red Cross, saying that you would surely die if you swam after you ate? There is absolutely no evidence of a link between eating before swimming and drowning, despite all of the warnings from the Red Cross, whose pants must be going up in flames on a daily basis.

ways he was right. I mean, my Volume Control Button drifted up on deafen years ago and my internal thermostat was stuck up on cremate for so long back when I was going through the change. For years, I was hot and loud, more like a Caribbean carnival really, than an actual human being. The menopause, I think, burnt out my entire Bodily Heating System so that one day, without warning, my temperature plummeted, and here I am now, constantly numb with the cold, my eyelashes are practically frosted, I'm ice-cold all the time, I'm going around like an aged Princess Elsa from *Frozen*. And of course I have always been a big girl for twelve, always eating my feelings, who knew they were so chock-a-block full of calories? Who knew envy and resentment weighed so much?

Right now I'm in that third stage of womanhood—you know the three stages: young, middle aged, and "Oh my God, Mary, you're lookin' good" (always said to me with a look of utter disbelief and surprise on the face of the sayers). Of course, I am looking good for someone who is 110 years of age, which is what everybody believes I must be by now because I've been playing old ladies since I was eighteen. I did a TV series in 1980 where I played a boarding-house mistress who was at least fifty, so that would make me how old now in 2026? Oh, I don't know, you do the math, I'm really, really bad at math. Right here does seems like a good time to mention that I probably do have some kind of ADHD or something, and that I find it impossible to stay on track. My brain dances around from thought to thought and sometimes I just have to follow it.*

---

* Does it seem now that everyone in the world has ADHD? Or is it just my crowd in the arts?

WHEN I WAS YOUNG, I ALWAYS THOUGHT I WAS TOO tall, too big, too loud, too everything. For years I was afraid to cut my hair short because once when I was about nine years old, a saucy little boy said to me, "What are you, a boy or a girl?" and that shattered me so completely that it stayed with me for decades. Was I really a girl? Or what was I? It was obvious to me at the time that there was something really wrong with me. I held on to that remark and was afraid to ever cut my hair short again until I was sixty-eight. Of course, as women, we are brought up to be insecure, aren't we? Always worried about how we present to the world, never quite good enough. Remember when we all longed to look like Twiggy? And if it wasn't Twiggy and being completely flat as a board, it was Kim Kardashian and having the biggest arse in the history of the world. There was always someone that you just did not look enough like but that you desperately wanted and needed to resemble. My eyes were always too small, my lips too thin, my waist too wide, my feet too big, I could never fit myself into that imaginary template of what a proper young woman should look like, or later, what a middle-aged woman in the late twentieth century should look like.

Oddly enough though, despite all indications to the contrary, when I was about forty-one I started to harbour a deeply hidden, secret hope that I might someday become beautiful. I remember thinking, "Look at Catherine Deneuve, she's exquisite, and she's fifty!" I magically thought myself into believing, or at least hoping, that I, too, might become exquisite by the time I was fifty. Of course, as some straight-talking friend pointed out to me, Catherine Deneuve was always beautiful, beautiful and exquisite long before she was fifty, and though they never said, they implied that I just wasn't.

Now, when I look at myself in pictures from ten years ago, I think, "Wow, I looked pretty good back then." But I remember that ten years ago, when that picture was being taken, I was thinking, "Oh my God, I am just hanging out over the top of these pants, and they used to fit me! Yuck! What's going on with my eyes, is that more wrinkles just in the middle of my cheeks? No one has wrinkles in the middle of their cheeks, do they?" Ten years ago, I couldn't believe how bad I looked, and suddenly ten years later, I'm thinking, "Wow I looked pretty good back then!" I started hoping that at some point I could get to that place where I could think, "Right now I look pretty good," and not have to wait ten years anymore to get there. And it finally happened.

Seriously, now when I look in the mirror, I have a brief and fleeting moment of despair, and I think, "Oh my God, I look like an old woman!" But that is immediately replaced with the comforting fact of "Well, that's what I am! I am an old woman." Thanks be to God, I think I've finally grown into myself.

Most days now, I'm lit up like a Christmas tree, suffused with a new sense of freedom. For the first time since I was about ten, I can finally wear what I want to wear, and I can at last break free of the beige prisons of those foundation garments. Oh, the Spanx, and the constricting crucifixion of the Cross Your Heart brassiere! The fella who came up with that should be shot. Of course it was designed by a man, it had to be, just the way it so relentlessly lifts and separates the girls till they are practically barking and whining, desperate to break free. Oh, you don't know incarceration until you're stuck inside a Cross Your Heart underwire push-up size 38D bra for twelve hours. You'd have to be El Chapo himself to break out of one of those things.

To tell you the truth, I just don't have the energy or the time left anymore for all the daily grooming that society requires for a woman. The endless flossing and plumping and grooming and gargling; abrading, moisturizing, deodorizing, plucking, shaving, lifting, waxing, firming, toning—and that's just to get me out the door of a morning, presentable enough to pass for an ordinary woman. I'm not even talking injections and derma-implants, or having the actual skin of your face cut away, or taking a bone from your leg to stick in your cheeks, or having your little toe savagely sawed off so you can fit your wide real woman's feet into those stiletto pointy-toed, "lay me down and do me" shoes. Never mind Adam's rib, what about those women who get their twelfth rib removed to give themselves that oh-so-desirable hourglass figure, all just so they can get a fella? Unbelievable.

Lucky for me, I have lived long enough that I have finally realized I'm probably never going to be the object of some fella's desire anymore. And right on the heels of that rather sobering knowledge came the delightful realization that I no longer wanted to be the object but had at last become the subject. The subject of my own life. And by the Lord dyin' jumpins', that is well worth getting old for.

Acknowledgements

Basil King, a Canadian Pastor and author, said, "Be bold and mighty forces will come to your aid." Sister Mary Nano always said I was a bold and saucy girl (she didn't mean it as a compliment), and always mighty forces have come to my aid.

This book would not exist without the help and encouragement of Gill Dawe—always an unstoppable force for good.

I owe a deep debt of gratitude to Kelly Lewis and to the wonderful Paul Hussey who rode in at the end and helped me navigate the profoundly confusing and upsetting editing system now in place across the publishing world.

Thank you to Rayanne Langdon, to the editorial staff at HarperCollins, and of course to Perry Zimel for all that he does.